give me 5

A teaching resource for children's and youth-church leaders

ollygoldenberg

Joining the Dots Distribution Ltd
Unit 1, Hargreaves Business Park
Hargreaves Road
Eastbourne
BN23 6QW

www.joiningthedotsdistribution.co.uk

ISBN 978-1-907080-34-0

Typesetting by Joanne Alderton

Contents

*"The only wrong teaching method
is the one that you use every week."*

Introduction

Give Me 5 is a compilation of material written over a ten-year period for use in churches working with children aged 5–16.

Just as we are encouraged to eat 5-a-day of fruit and vegetables for healthy living, so we need our spiritual 5-a-day with God for healthy, spiritual lives. Every week our children need to be built up in five key areas, known as the 5 Ws, if they are going to grow spiritually strong:

1. **Welcome** – "Hi, how are you doing?" Ice-breaker and team-building ideas which build a sense of fellowship and belonging; this time also includes a chance to check on the welfare of each member of the group.

2. **Worship** – "God is great." To lead the children and young people to go further than just singing songs, and worship God from their hearts.

3. **Word** – "Let's learn about God." Studying God's Word and preparing to live it out in everyday life.

4. **Warfare** – "Let's talk to God." Leading the children to engage in the spiritual realm through prayer.

5. **Witness** – "You can tell others about God." Encouraging the children and young people to look out from the group to those who don't know God.

Our spiritual diet for the children should give equal weight to all five of these areas if we are going to grow balanced believers. Coming up with creative, age-appropriate ways of developing the children and young people in all these areas week after week is easier said than done. As a default position most of us end up giving the most time to the areas we feel the most comfortable in, but in so doing we neglect other areas and so hinder the development of the disciples under our care. This is where Give Me 5 comes in.

Give Me 5 has over 100 activity ideas for each of these five areas, grouped by activity type. There is no one method that will work for every group in every setting. Although you can use each idea as described I hope that the suggestions in this book will also serve as a springboard for other ideas. You may look at one and find it unsuitable for your group, but with a bit of adapting it may provide the inspiration for something that will be just what you were looking for, without you having to start with a blank sheet of paper.

For ease of reading we have generally used the word 'children' to refer to both children and young people. Most of the activities in this book will work across the whole age range of children's and youth ministry, requiring either minor or no adaptations.

As a rule of thumb I suggest you set aside two hours to prepare for the Sunday session – an hour to get the activities ready and an hour to spend in prayer so that the children and young people under your care will really meet with God and be changed by His Word. Prayer and preparation are the keys to a successful Sunday session.

My thanks goes to the many group leaders at Kensington Temple down through the years who have road tested these ideas. Special thanks goes to Nancy Fernandez for her assistance in compiling this book. Thanks also to the fantastically supportive team at Joining the Dots. Thanks to Kevin Whomes, Joanne Alderton and Rebecca Henning for improving the layout and ironing out the mistakes. Any errors that remain are of course my own. Special thanks to Jonathan Budgen for your friendship, wisdom, love and support to our whole family as we travel on the journey.

I hope this material will prove to be a valuable resource in bringing a variety of teaching styles to the children as we seek to train them in the ways of God.

Olly Goldenberg

Icons

Each activity in this book is labelled with icons to help you find the best activities to use each week.

The following icons show the amount of preparation that is required for each session:

No preparation required (perfect for when you find yourself leading a group with no notice).

Activities that will require less than a couple of minutes of preparation.

More preparation will be needed. It may mean you need to make something, buy something, or simply think about how you will make the activity work.

Additional icons provide further information relating to the activities:

Our favourites for helping to develop the children as disciples.

Require extra materials that you will need to bring to the group.

Suitable for children under seven. Most of these activities also work well for older children and teenagers who will love the retro experience of some of the games.

Suited to Christmas, Easter or the start of a new year.

Welcome

Contents

Introduction

The Welcome time of the group is about developing fellowship between the members of the group. By allowing them to get to know each other better, they can grow together in the things of the kingdom. As they grow up together we are developing that feeling of family; of serving God together.

Our group members should go beyond the Sunday times to caring for each other during the week. After all, this is a key part of what Church is about. As you share together on a Sunday, do try and bring a concern for the wider week into the group.

Beware, this is not supposed to be the 'fun' part of the group, before we get on to the 'serious' part of meeting with God. If all parts of the group are run in their fullness then everyone will have fun in all the sections. After all, what greater fun is there than being in God's presence, worshipping Him?

So allow the time for deep, God-centred friendships to develop and encourage a godly attitude towards one another in all of the interactions during this time.

Debates/Discussions

1. Life-changing Faith

Aim: To get the group to understand that a faith-filled life is a blessing.

Get the group to talk about the 'challenges' they are facing (e.g. handling a bully at school, completing assignments on time, letting go of a comfort blanket).

Ask the group how they have tried to overcome challenges in the past; ask them how they would now approach them with faith.

Make sure everybody understands how their faith can change the situations.

Pray with the children.

2. WWJD

Ask each group member to share something bad/sad that happened to them in the last week which they felt was not fair. Ask them what they did about it. Then discuss "What Would Jesus Do?" in each of these situations.

3. Faith And Prayer

- Discuss in groups examples of when you prayed and got the answers you wanted.

- Discuss examples of when you prayed and did not get what you wanted.

- Discussion question – Why did your faith seem to work sometimes and not at other times?

  Discussion answers – There are many reasons but here are three:

  You were asking for the wrong things.

  It may not be the right time for you to have it.

  God simply has a better plan.

4. Bring And Share

Get each group member to bring some clothes or fashion accessories to share (they could be modern, dated or simply unusual). Have fun sharing together. You could also bring photos from several decades ago to see how fashions have changed.

5. Taking Ownership

Ask group members to suggest some Welcome ideas to be used in the group in the coming weeks. This will encourage them to be involved in setting some direction for the group and will help to develop a sense of ownership.

6. Does Faith Make You Do Crazy Things?

Tell the following story: "This guy named Peter and a bunch of his fishermen friends went fishing. They fished all night and caught nothing. They were tired, cold and hungry. The sea was getting rough so they decided to go back home. Up comes Jesus and tells them to throw their nets over the other side of the boat and they will catch lots of fish. Hey, He was not even a fisherman. What does He know about fish?"

- Your big question: "If you were Peter, what would you do?" Let the group come up with a number of different possibilities.

- At the end of the discussion, tell them that God may ask them to do impossible or strange things. We simply need to have faith in Him and do it. He is always right.

7. Question Time

Bring a ball to the group. Throw the ball at someone and ask them a question about their life. When they have answered the question they get to throw the ball on to someone else and ask a question.

8. Market Traders

Choose two vocal members of your group and tell them that you would like them to be market traders. They need to shout out to sell their goods. Salesmen have the art of selling something you don't want at a price you can't afford! However these salesmen have a difficult task: One is trying to sell heaven; the other is trying to sell hell. Let the other group members chip in with ideas when those speaking run out of sales points.

9. Holy Ghost Story Time

Get the group to share stories they have heard of how God has moved at different times in history. Also ask them to share things from their own lives.

10. Freestyle

Use the time to let the group integrate and interact with each other as they choose.

11. My Christmas

Divide the group into pairs. Encourage them to share their Christmas traditions. Do they have any funny memories or genuine disasters from this time?

12. Job Descriptions

Bring pictures that represent various professions. Talk about what those people sacrifice to do that job. Possible professions include fireman, policeman, doctor, teacher.

13. Toilet-paper Surprise

Welcome the group at the door while holding a roll of toilet paper. Tell the group that they can take as many sheets as they need, but don't explain the purpose. When the group begins, instruct them to write one thing about themselves on each sheet. When students are finished, they can read their toilet paper out loud.

14. Musical Tunes

Play a sample of Christian music from across the decades. Discuss as a group what they think of the different types of music.

15. Ball Boy

Bring a ball to the group. Throw the ball from one person to another. The person who is holding the ball has to tell the rest of the group something about their week.

16. You Have to Hear This

Divide the group into pairs.

One person tells the other about an exciting experience they've had and why it was important to them. After about five minutes bring the group back together to share some of the things they have heard. One person from each pair can share with the rest of the group what the other person told them, explaining:

• Why they think it was a great experience.

• If they would like to have the same thing happen to them.

17. Wrong Impression

Show the children a picture of a man pushing a woman onto the street. Get the children to talk about what they would do if they saw this happening. Then unfold the picture to reveal that he is actually grabbing her to pull her away from a lorry coming near.

Alternatively get the children to act a mime of the following: Ask three children to act out the scene of a man pulling a woman across a road and she is resisting. Only the one pulling can see a lorry coming. Have the rest of the group discuss what they are seeing and note the various deductions. After the discussion, have the driver drive past and get their reactions again. Compare how it was possible to come to the wrong conclusions.

Or start the group with something dramatic. E.g. have someone run through the room 'wrecking' the place. After it has happened explain it was all a set up, and that they have been witnesses to it. Get each of the children to write an account of what happened and then compare accounts. Discuss how they all saw the same thing, but had different interpretations of it.

18. A Different Culture

Get the group to put themselves in someone else's shoes. For younger children you may want to bring along costumes and food from different cultures so that they can imagine what it is like. For teenagers you could get them to imagine what it would be like to live without food or to be the prime minister of England.

19. History

Get the group to work together, over the course of a month, to produce a history of Israel. Each aspect of Israel's history could be shown using pictures only, starting with Abraham's call through to the future prophecies. By discovering more about the nation of Israel it will be easier to understand the context of individual stories.

20. Those with Less

Talk about how we can bless those with less than us this month.

21. For Christmas I Want

Get the group to share what they want for Christmas. Then speak about the value of things that last. They will grow out of toys (do they still want what they wanted three years ago!) but God is there forever.

22. Family Fun

Invite a parent to join your group this week. Interview them to find out what family life is like from a parent's point of view.

23. Really, Really Want

Suppose you see a poor man outside your church door and he asks for help. Which of the following would you give and why?

- Money
- Clothes
- A Bible
- Cigarettes
- Food
- Beer

24. Right or wrong

Afghanistan is a very poor country. It is alleged that it was people who trained and lived in Afghanistan who were responsible for the tragedy in America on 11 September 2001. In the current war between America and the Taliban, America is supplying food as well as bombing the country. As a Christian, what is your view on this? Should America be doing both, only one, or neither. Why?

25. Faith or Foolishness

Which of the following is faith and which is not? Ask the group to decide whether each scenario is an example of faith or foolishness. (Why not make up your own scenarios?)

- You are late for school and there are many cars on the road. You decide to cross the road by faith instead of waiting for the traffic light to change.

- There is a shortage of money at home this month. You decide to pray that God will provide some because God says in His Word that if He provides for the birds of the air, He will provide even more for us.

- Because there is no money at home, you decide to go to Tesco and pick up all you need. You then begin to pray, as you leave the shop without paying, that you will not be stopped by the store security.

Faith can look like foolishness but it must start with a word from God and will never go against the moral principles in the Bible. Faith must be used with wisdom and honesty.

26. Debate

Ask for a show of hands from those who agree with the following statement:

"I am not sure what the church does with my money so I am not going to put any money in the offering."

Now divide the group into two teams – those who agree with the statement in one and those who do not in another.

Both teams must have the same number of members. If there are more on one team than the other, the extras become an audience. If all the people are on one side then ask some of them to argue on the other side.

Set debating rules and time, then let them debate their opinion.

Welcome

27. Movie Mania

Get the children to talk about some of the films that they have seen and which bits they liked.

28. Discussing Worship

Ask the group to explain the kind of worship they enjoy. Which songs help them really to worship God? Is there a particular style of worship song that they like or dislike?

29. Take And Share

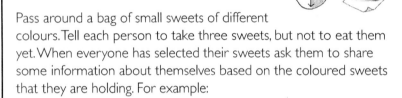

Pass around a bag of small sweets of different colours. Tell each person to take three sweets, but not to eat them yet. When everyone has selected their sweets ask them to share some information about themselves based on the coloured sweets that they are holding. For example:

- If they have a *red* sweet they have to share a piece of *personal* information (name, subjects studied, school, age).

- If they have a *yellow* sweet they have to share something about their *family* (parents, brothers, sisters, pets).

- If they have an *orange* sweet this is a *free* category – they can use it to say something fun about themselves or they don't have to say anything.

- If they have a *green* sweet they have to share something about their *life* with God (a favourite Bible verse, something God said to them, how God has changed them).

- If they have a *purple* sweet they have to share something about one of their *hobbies or other interests* (sports, dancing, talents).

30. Do You Know Me?

Test your group on how much they know about each other by asking a list of simple questions about each member. If they know very little then you can set that straight by getting them to ask each other questions.

31. Testimonies

Ask the group to share testimonies of how God has worked through them and answered their prayers in the past week.

32. The Best And the Worst

Get each person in the group to share the best day of their life and the worst day of their life so far.

33. Debate

Hold a debate on the following topic: "The world would be better off without leaders." Play devil's advocate in the debate to keep people thinking, until they see the value of leadership.

34. Close Friends

Discuss what you can do as a group to develop friendships beyond the weekly meeting together.

35. My Name Means

Get the group to share what their names mean (you could even make up a names dictionary for your group with all their names and the meanings in one place). Look also at the meaning of 'Israel'. If people do not know what their names mean you may want to use a book of names or an internet resource.

36. I Can Convince You

Split the group into two groups or into pairs.

One group will be the supporters; the others will be the non-supporters. Give the supporters a topic, for example: I am football crazy; I support Arsenal; I support Manchester United; I like David Beckham's new hairstyle; I hate pets; Britney Spears' music is my favourite; Craig David's music is my favourite; I like going to church; I don't like going to church.

Ask for a show of hands from those who like each of the above. Match a supporter with a non-supporter. The supporter has to try and convince the non-supporter to change their mind and become a supporter by telling them all that is good about their choice of topic above.

After this exercise get each group to give feedback, to see if anyone has managed to change another person's mind. How difficult was it?

Winning arguments does not get people saved; we need the Spirit of God to show people the truth.

37. Thief's Profile

In small teams, see who can come up with the longest list of words to describe a thief. For example: uncaring, selfish, desperate.

38. Smelly Feet

Suppose someone walks up to you and says, "Could you wash my feet? I have been walking for a long time. My feet are tired, smelly and dirty." What would you do and why?

39. Debate

Get the group to debate the following: 'Capital punishment should be brought back in our country.'

40. Rhyme all the Time

Get the group to discuss a topic, but tell them everything they say has to rhyme.

41. How Fashionable

Bring some fashion magazines and music magazines and ask the group what they would wear, buy, or listen to. As they discuss this among themselves sit back and learn more about your group!

Active

42. Puzzle Pact

Before the group begins take two or three pictures and cut them up so that there are enough pieces for each person to have one. Put the pieces into a bag. On arrival each person can then take a piece of a puzzle from the bag. Lay out any spare pieces on the floor for anyone to grab. When you say "GO!" each person has to locate the missing pieces of their puzzle to complete it. The first group to complete the puzzle wins.

43. Arm Wrestling

Have the children arm-wrestle each other. Then talk about what it is like to win, and what it is like to lose.

44. Colour Coordinated

Get the group to look at their clothes and then gather objects from the room that are the same colour (or even the same shade) as their clothes. The person who gets the most objects in the time allowed is the winner. Then see who can be the first to put all the objects back where they got them from. The first person to do this is also the winner.

45. Creative Scavenge

Get the group to collect things God has made. Gather them together and look at them. Thank Him for each item.

46. Opposites

As you call out instructions each person has to do the opposite of what you tell them to. For example: if you tell them to stand up they should sit down; if you tell them to make noise they should be quiet.

47. Hat Trick

Form a circle. Put a hat on one person. He has to place the hat on to the next person's head without using hands, arms, teeth or legs (for younger children you may want to allow the use of teeth!). You could bring two hats and divide the group into two, to have a competition.

48 Tastionary

Each person takes it in turns to be blindfolded and taste different foods to see if they can work out what it is. If you have expert tasters why not try doing it with baby food! Don't forget to check for allergies and intolerances with parents/guardians first.

49. Colour Magnet

Give each member of the group the name of a colour (use between three and five colours depending on the size of the group). Then each person has to link up with those who have the same colour as them. The first time they are not allowed to say the name of the colour they are. Repeat the game but this time they are not even allowed to talk as they try to find out who has the same colour as them.

50. Hide It

Make a list of objects and hide them around the room before the session begins. See how long it takes for all the objects to be found.

51. Sherrards

Divide the group into two teams. They have to act out titles of films, songs and books without using any words. Limit the time for each person so that everyone can have a go. The winning team is the one that guesses the most correctly.

52. Musical Games

Play a traditional musical game. For example, musical chairs, musical statues, or musical bumps. Why not have a prize for the winner?

53. Tied Football

If you have space, why not play a game of football with a twist? After picking two teams, the players divide into pairs (one player from each side). In each pair, tie one leg to that of the other person. Now try to play the game as normal. See how the teams are able to play as they try to get and pass the ball with the pairs pulling in opposite directions. This can lead on to a great discussion on the importance of unity.

54. Relay Races

Run relay races with the children (e.g. three-legged races, hopping races, skipping races, running races). Young people like to go back to their childhood and do this one too!

55. What Is the Value?

Bring balls of different colours (or coloured sheets of paper) to the group. Split the group into two teams. Tell the group that each colour is worth a different number of points but do not tell them how much each one is worth at this stage. Each team collects the balls one at a time, to try and gather as many balls as possible in the available time. At the end, tell them how many points each coloured ball is worth, then add up the points to find out the winner.

56. Act It

Write each part of the fruit of the Spirit on a piece of paper and put it into a bag. Give two people a scene to act out, for example a child coming home late from school. As they are acting select a piece of paper from the bag and give it to one of the actors. The actor then has to show this aspect of the fruit as they carry on the scene. For example, if they are given the card 'love', everything their character does needs to be loving. Change the actors around as the sketch develops so that everyone has a go.

Alternatively, watch a popular cartoon together, and see which of the fruit of the Spirit the cartoon characters display (and which they don't!).

57. Stay Serious

Sit the group in a circle. The aim of the game is to try and make one another laugh. The first person should turn to the person on their right and say: "It is a sad and solemn day *brother/sister NAME.*"

The person replies: "It is indeed *brother/sister NAME.*"

The first person then replies: "It is indeed."

The second person then turns to the person on the right and repeats the same conversation. If anyone laughs, they are out. Once the group has remembered the words they will have fun trying to make each other laugh whilst keeping a straight face themselves.

58. Hold It

Find out who can
hold their breath the longest.

59. Power to Push

Get the members of your group to stand in a door frame
one at a time. They should start with their hands by their sides and
then gradually lift their hands, keeping their arms straight, until their
hands touch the edge of the doorframe. At this point get them to
push outwards against the walls of the doorframe, as hard as they
can, for 90 seconds. After this time they should step forward. They
will experience their hands drifting upwards. Try it yourself before
group as it will be easier to explain to the members, (just make
sure your neighbours aren't watching you do it, otherwise they
may think you're a bit weird!).

60. Panic And Pray

Get the group together and tell them
you are going to talk through a day in the life of
Femi Umbabo. As you talk through the day, get the
group members to act out what Femi is doing.
During the course of the day have a number of
things go wrong (e.g. he discovers he has left his
books at home when he gets to school). Then say
he started to panic. On this word everyone
should panic! When you shout out the word 'pray'
they have to drop to their knees and pray.

61. Faith Interview

You will need four volunteers for this
role play of a television interview. One will be
an interviewer and three will be guests. Each
of the guests should think of a faith story
based on their own personal experience.

The interviewer should invite and introduce
each guest to the audience. Each guest should
sit in the 'hot seat' and tell the story of how
they applied faith in a situation in their life,
answering whatever questions the interviewer
throws at them.

62. Blessings of Cheerful Giving

Bring a box of sweets to the class. Give half of the group
sweets, but ask them not to eat them. Instead they have to give them all to
those who do not have any. These people are then allowed to eat the sweets.

Talk about how it feels to be in the different situations: to go without, when
others have some; to sacrifice something for those who do not have anything;
suddenly to receive something unexpected at someone else's expense.

At the end make sure everybody ends up having some sweets. Ensure they
understand that when we give to God, He makes sure He blesses us abundantly.

Welcome

63. No Encounters

Ask everybody to stand up and walk around the room. Tell them they are not allowed to bump into each other. As time goes by reduce the area in which they are allowed to walk. If two people bump into each other they are out.

64. Getting to Know You

Stick up three letters around the room (A, B and C). Then ask the group a number of questions with three answers (A, B or C). They should then go and stand by the different letters around the room. E.g. Do you like chocolate? A=yes, B=no, C=not sure; How many brothers do you have? A=0, B=1, C=2 or more.

65. Stop, Wait, Go

When you say "go", everyone can run around the room.

When you say "wait", everybody has to walk.

When you say "stop", everyone has to stand still.

Anyone who is too slow to respond is out.

66. Who Is Faster?

Seat two people back to back on chairs, two metres apart. Place a piece of string on the floor so that each end of the string sits between the feet of the players. Tie a bag of sweets to the middle of the string.

When you say "go", each player has to get up, run around the other person's chair and return to their seat. Once sitting down again they can grab the end of the string and pull it to get hold of the prize before their opponent does.

67. Act And React

Get the group to act out a scene that lasts about one minute. (With a larger group you may want to divide them into smaller groups.) When they have done this get them to act the scene again, with the same words, but this time each person has to act in as sad a way as possible (even if it is completely inappropriate for the scene). Repeat the scene again, but this time, as happily as possible. Other ways could include: melodramatically, tragically, artificially, or angrily.

68. Community Action

Work together, as a group, to make a list of needy people in the community and to think about what can be done to help them. For example, the elderly, the homeless, the lonely.

Welcome

69. Just for Fun

Call out a number of different rhyming commands that the group have to follow: "Run just for fun", "Jump on the hump", "Hop till you drop", "Walk don't talk". When they have got the hang of this only say the second part of the rhyme, but they still have to do the full action.

70. Fruit Salad

Make a circle of chairs with a clear space in the middle for people to move around in. Put out one less chair than the number of people in the group and ask each person to sit on a chair. Go around the circle giving each person the name of a fruit, until every person has the name of a fruit that they need to remember (use between three and five fruits, depending on the size of the group).

Stand in the centre of the circle and call out the name of one of the fruits. Everyone who is that fruit must get up and quickly move to a different chair; everyone else stays sitting down. When people are changing seats, you can sit on one of the empty seats.

One person will be left without a chair. They then get to be the caller and have to try and poach a seat. To get everyone to move all at once, the person in the middle calls out "fruit salad".

Once everyone understands the game, speed up the time between claiming the chairs and calling out the next fruit.

71. Line Up

Get the group to make a line starting with the biggest and going down to the smallest. It may be height order, shoe size, age, hair length, or anything else of your choosing. Alternatively get them to stand in groups based on things like year group at school, number of siblings or favourite subject.

To make it harder get them to do this but without talking.

72. Alternative Snowball Fight

Bring loads of scrap paper to the group and get the children to screw each piece up into a ball. Split the group into two teams, one on each side of the room and let them have an indoor snowball fight, throwing the 'snowballs' at each other.

73. Crossing the River

Place a number of folded newspapers on the floor with spaces in between. These represent rocks across a river. The group has to try and cross the river without getting their feet wet. Each person can cross one at a time, blindfolded. Give them two chances to get their feet wet then they are disqualified. Change the position of the 'rocks' from time to time.

74. Get to the Front

Get the whole group to stand in a line. Choose a category, e.g. cutlery, animals, subjects at school, boys' names. Starting at the back of the line, each person takes it in turns to give the name of something in this category without repeating anything that has been said before. When the person at the front has had their turn, start at the back again.

If anyone hesitates or repeats something that has already been said they move to the back of the line. You can then start again with a new category.

75. The Mostest

Let each member of the group take it in turns doing as many press-ups as they can, while everybody else counts for them. The person who does the most press-ups is the winner.

76. Move On

Get the group to sit in a circle and call out instructions to them such as: "If you are wearing blue move one seat to the left," or, "If you have ever eaten duck move three spaces to the right." If someone is already sitting on the chair that they are moving to, then they sit on that person's (or those people's) lap(s).

77. Time Bomb

Bring a soft ball to the group. Have the group members throw it to each other and catch it. If the ball is dropped and touches the ground, start counting down from ten, as they continue throwing the ball between themselves. When you reach the end of the countdown, the person who touched the ball last is out.

78. Keep Fit

Do keep-fit exercises. As you do them, pretend to be different people: The queen of England, your granny, a toddler, an Olympic sportsman, etc.

79. Get Fit

Do an aerobics routine to music.

80. Swing Ball

Build a 'swing ball' by tying a length of thick string to the handles of a bag filled with a large, light ball (such as a football), a cushion, or clothes. The players stand in a circle around a central person, who holds the swing ball. The central person starts to swing the 'swing ball' round and round, keeping it level and about 40cm off the ground.

At the command 'Go!' all the players must step into the path of the 'ball' and start jumping over it as it swings around. If the 'ball' touches a player they are out. Continue play until only one player is left.

Welcome

81. Out We Go

Take your group out to the park for a session of fun. Make sure it is sunny, you have parents' permission, and sufficient adult leaders for the outing.

82. Guess Who?

Give each group member a clean sheet of white, unlined paper, on which they can write three to five unique things about themselves. Make sure they do NOT put their name on it. Next, have them screw the paper up into a ball.

Allow them one full minute to throw the balls at each other! When one minute is up, have them locate the 'snowball' nearest to them, unfold it and try to guess whose it is.

83. Human Taco

Stick a card with the name of a taco ingredient on to the back of everyone's shirt. Explain the correct order of ingredients in a Human Taco: shell, meat, cheese, lettuce, tomato, salsa.

Then call out, "It's taco time!" Each person has to find out what ingredient they are and then club together with other people to form a complete Human Taco.

84. The Broom Dance

You need a broom and an odd number of people to play. If you have an extra person they can help start and stop the music. The players all take partners. The extra person dances with the broom. When the music suddenly stops, all the players must change partners. The person with the broomstick drops it and grabs a partner. The player who is left without a partner picks up the broom and dances with it until the music stops again.

85. Throw it, Catch it

Bring a ball to group. Have the group members throw it to each other. If someone drops it they must kneel on one knee. If they catch it they can stand back up again. If they drop it again they kneel on both knees. If they catch it they go back to one knee.

Penalties are as follows: kneel on one knee; kneel on both knees; kneel on both knees and only one hand; kneel on both knees and both hands; out of the game.

86. Go And Do

Prepare together a time when you will do something different during your weekly time together. For example, you could visit an old-people's home. The preparation for this could take place as part of both the Welcome and the Witness times of the group. Once you are prepared actually go out and do it. Remember that you will need to have parental permission and ensure you have enough adults to look after those who will be with you.

People Bingo

87. People Bingo

Give a copy of the sheet below to each person. They then have to complete the sheet with names of people in the room who match each description. They are not allowed to use the same name more than twice.

Has ridden on an aeroplane.	Likes to eat French Fries.	Is wearing pink.	Went to a different school last year.	Has one sister.
(1 point)	(1 point)	(1 point)	(1 point)	(1 point)
Wears glasses.	Likes to eat pizza.	Has four letters in his/her first name.	Has a last name that starts with an 'S'.	Is wearing blue.
(1 point)	(1 point)	(1 point)	(1 point)	(1 point)
Takes the bus to school.	Likes to read.	Knows what 4+9 is.	Has a dog.	Has brown hair.
(2 points)	(2 points)	(2 points)	(2 points)	(2 points)
Has a computer at home.	Has been on television.	Has been to the zoo.	Has more than six letters in his or her first name.	Will not eat meat for lunch today.
(3 points)	(3 points)	(3 points)	(3 points)	(3 points)

Craft/Creative

88. Our Group

Work together to make up a poem about your group.

89. A Poem About Me

Get each group member to write a poem about themselves.

The first line is their first name.

The second line is three words that describe themselves.

The third line is three things they like.

The fourth line is three things they do not like.

The fifth line is three films they have seen.

The sixth line is three fears they have.

The seventh line is three things they like about God.

The eighth line is two goals they have in life.

The ninth line is a place they would like to visit.

The tenth line is their last name.

The following week read the poems aloud, leaving out the first and last line. See if people can guess which poem belongs to whom.

90. Crossing the Bridge

Split into groups of three or four. Give each group some paper clips and A4 sheets of paper. Tell them to construct a bridge that spans at least 15cm. Judge each bridge on strength, length and beauty.

91. The Days We Are In

Get the group to make a collage entitled 'The world we live in today'. Bring newspapers and magazines for the group to cut up and paste together to make the collage.

92. My Jesus

Split into groups of three. Provide some drawing equipment. Let them discuss what they think Jesus looks like and draw what they finally decide on. Each group can then share their drawing, and their reasoning behind it, with the rest of the group. Remember to explain that we don't have any photos of Jesus, but this exercise helps to remind us of different aspects of Jesus' character. Compare their pictures to the description of Jesus in Revelation 1:12-16.

93. In God's Path

Tell everyone to make a picture, either in groups or individually, to show how we need to stay on God's path. For example, it may be a collage of two paths, or a picture of people choosing to do right or wrong things. Let them be creative in their expression of this aspect of Christian living.

94. The Low Down

Create a rap of the Ten Commandments. Alternatively the children can present each Commandment as a freeze-frame picture, where members of the group freeze in mid-action to depict each one.

95. Easter Project

Plan an Easter project, such as making Easter cards, an Easter game, or an Easter scene as a group. This project could run over a number of weeks.

96. Newsletter

Take time in the group to prepare something for the church newsletter, reporting on what God is doing. Alternatively create your own group newsletter.

97. Tropical Beach

Work together as a group to make a beach scene. Use various materials to make the different parts of the beach. E.g. clear plastic for the water, sandpaper for the sand. As you do it, discuss what their ideal dream in life is and relate this to God's call on their lives.

98. Getting to Know A Bible Character

Take a Bible character involved in the teaching for the week. Sketch out different scenes from the Bible story (or print them from the internet) and have the children colour the pictures in, ready for when you come to share the story from the Bible.

99. Christmas Play

Create a Christmas play, or rehearse a song together, to show to the parents. Encourage the children not to perform it, but to use it to minister the Christmas message. Make sure that they not only rehearse but also pray, in preparation for how God is going to use them. Don't forget afterwards to pass any feedback from the adults back to them so they can hear how God used them.

100. Make A Festive Scene

Get the children to build a model of the nativity scene. They can use Plasticine for the characters, or you can make them all out of paper. Use a box for the stable and shredded paper, or straw, for the hay.

101. The Cross

Create a giant cross out of paper. Remind everybody what Jesus did for us on the cross. Get them to think about where on the cross they would like to write their name, and why. For example: in the centre to be close to Jesus' heart; at His feet to show that I worship Him because of what He did; by His hands because I know He holds me in His hands and keeps me safe. Once they have explained their reason let them write their name on the cross in that place.

102. Family Photo

Ask everyone to draw a picture of their family.

103. Prepare It

Get the group to prepare puppets, and a puppet sketch, for the Bible story. Let them make up the script using the Bible and expressing their own creativity.

104. Super Leader

Work together as a group to create a picture of what a super leader looks like, e.g. with a large brain to work out problems; super sight to see things other people miss; heart to love people with. Ask the children to compare themselves to this leader and see how God is getting them ready to lead their friends to Him. Compare yourself to this leader too, to show them that we are all works in progress!

105. Sheep And Shepherd

Let each person make a sheep, using various materials such as card, cotton wool, wool, pens. They can then each place their sheep around the good shepherd, knowing that the shepherd will take care of them, no matter what.

106. Me!

Bring some large sheets of paper to group (backing paper used for decorating is nice and cheap!). Get each person to lie on the paper, while someone else draws round them. When everyone has their shape they can write on it, or draw on it, the things that they would like in their life.

107. Faith Report

Create a newspaper publication entitled 'The Daily Faith Report'. Get the group to write articles and draw photo-like pictures for the newspaper, detailing historical people of faith and also up-to-date faith examples from their own lives.

108. Invited

Get each person to make an invitation for an upcoming church event, to use to invite their friends along.

109. The Gathering Town

Use boxes and other recycled materials to make a city with houses, shops, a school, a church building, and a football stadium. When it is complete create people and then put them wherever people can gather to talk to Jesus.

110. Our Story

Take photos of each person in the group the week before (remember to gain permission from parents and guardians). Bring the photos with you and make a storybook up using their pictures.

111. The World Today

Create a collage of newspaper clippings describing the various events that have been taking place in the world over the past few weeks. With all that is happening, we need to look to God.

112. Drawing It Blind

Blindfold each member the group and then get them to draw a picture of an animal. Then, see how they do if someone guides them with their drawing. Compare the two pictures and talk about how the Holy Spirit is there to guide us in our everyday lives.

113. A Picture Is Worth 1000 Words

Get each person to draw a picture that illustrates a Gospel truth.

114. Build A Bridge

Give the group some straws and newspaper and instruct them to make a bridge capable of holding a small weight and crossing a certain distance. For larger groups split the participants into small groups with around three people in each. This activity can be used to introduce the concept of intercession as a bridge between God and others.

115. Our Group!

Using a digital camera, or a camera phone, take a photo of the whole group (make sure you have the permission of parents/guardians). You can use this during the week to make a card of the group. The following week they can discuss different ways to use it: for decoration, to pray for the people in the group or to invite friends to the group. Follow through on some of their suggestions.

116. Thank-you Letters

Get each person to write a thank-you letter, or make a thank-you card, to give to somebody. The letters should thank people not for something material that they have given, but for loving and helping us.

117. Create A Puzzle

Get the group to draw a picture (or use a pre-drawn picture). Mount it on card and then cut it into pieces to make a puzzle. The older the group, the more pieces you can cut it into. The group can then try to put the picture back together again.

118. News Report

Take an item in the news that concerns Israel this week. Show it to the group, and get them to re-write the news item, but this time from God's perspective.

119. Thank-you Card

Get the group to make cards, or write poems, or indeed use any other creative way they may choose, to express their love and their thanks to their parents.

120. Bible Scroll

Get each person to make a scroll on which they can write notes on each week's teaching. They can then unwind it to remind themselves of what they have learnt.

121. Friendship Bracelets

Make friendship bracelets. These are special bracelets which you put beads on to and give to a friend as a sign of your friendship with them.

122. Symbols

Explain how in ancient days stories were written down not with words, but with pictures. These would be drawn on cave walls, or on the ground. Get the group to put the Bible story of the week into pictures on the wall. (Don't forget to stick paper on to the wall first, otherwise the caretaker will probably not be pleased with you!)

123. Dart Test

Tell the following story, or repeat the lesson below:

A young lady named Sally relates an experience she had in a seminary class given by her teacher, Dr Smith. She says that Dr Smith was known for his elaborate object lessons. One particular day, Sally walked into the seminary and knew they were in for a fun day. On the wall was a big target and on a nearby table were many darts. Dr Smith told the students to draw a picture of someone that they disliked or someone who had made them angry, and he would allow them to throw darts at the person's picture.

Sally's friend drew a picture of the girl who had stolen her boyfriend. Another friend drew a picture of his little brother. Sally drew a picture of a former friend, putting a great deal of detail into her drawing, even drawing pimples on the face. Sally was pleased with the overall effect she had achieved.

The class lined up and began throwing darts. Some of the students threw their darts with such force that their targets were ripping apart. Sally looked forward to her turn and was filled with disappointment when Dr Smith, because of time limits, asked the students to return to their seats. As Sally sat thinking about how angry she was because she hadn't had a chance to throw any darts at her target, Dr Smith began removing the target from the wall.

Underneath the target was a picture of Jesus. A hush fell over the room as each student viewed the mangled picture of Jesus; holes and jagged marks covered His face and His eyes were pierced. Dr Smith said only these words …"In as much as ye have done it unto the least of these my brethren, ye have done it unto Me." (Matthew 25:40.) No other words were necessary; the tear-filled eyes of the students focused only on the picture of Christ.

124. The Garden of Eden

Get the group to think about Creation and to make a model of the Garden of Eden with all the wonderful things that God made in it. You could do it in 2D with pictures or in 3D with modelling clay and other craft resources.

125. Money Boxes

Decorate some empty bottles or jars to transform them into money boxes. Explain that these boxes can be used to collect money for the poor. The children could put in all the copper coins they get and see how much they can raise in a three-month period. Choose a suitable charity to donate the money to.

126. Build A Church Building

You may want to do this Welcome activity over a number of weeks. Using cardboard and other materials get the children to work together to build a pretend church. They may want to put in lots of detail (such as people inside and a garden outside). Be as creative as you dare! Remind the group that the Church is not a building but the Church is the people (we do not go to church – we are the Church!).

Alternatively why not make a model temple based on I Kings 6?

127. Making Music

Create shakers and other musical instruments to be used in the worship time. For example, a yoghurt pot filled with lentils and covered over with cardboard stuck down well makes a great shaker.

128. Your Family Tree

Show the group how to draw a family tree of the different people in their family. See how many people you can put on the tree. For younger children you may want to have a basic template already prepared for them (showing where to place parents, uncles and aunts, etc.)

129. Make A Dream Board

A dream board is a board where you write or draw things that you want to see happen as a group. Start by decorating the board together with clouds and a title. Then spend time listening to God and praying to find out what dreams to put on the board.

130. God Rules the World

Get the group to make a montage of the world with a huge crown over the top of it. Explain that this shows that God rules over the whole world.

131. Dressing Up

Bring in some costumes, including a sheet, in which the children can dress up. Remember the costumes do not need to be perfect – their creativity will fill in the details! For example a white sheet could belong to a Roman leader, an angel or a priest. See how many different characters they can create out of the clothing you provide.

Welcome

132. Storybook

Work together to make a montage or a storybook of the story for the week. This can be a great team-building exercise if done in small groups, or you can use it to find out what each person sees as the key points of the story.

133. Fact File

Create a group fact file, with a page devoted to each member of the group. As well as the obvious basic details of name and age, include things like favourite food, favourite verse and other quirky facts. You may even want to include a photo of each of your group members or perhaps a group photo for the front cover of the fact file (make sure you have the permission of parents/guardians if you choose to do this).

134. Links in the Chain

Give each person a piece of A4 paper and get them to fold it into five equal segments. Then ask everyone to draw a picture of somebody's (or something's) head in the top fifth of the paper. They should then fold over their segment and pass the paper on to the next person.

On the second segment they can all draw a neck, fold the segment so their drawing cannot be seen and pass it on.

On the third segment they can draw a body and arms, and then pass it on.

On the fourth segment they can draw legs, and then pass it on.

On the fifth segment they can draw feet.

They can then unfold the picture to see the finished creation. Ask them if it looks like anyone they know!

Hot tip: Encourage them, as they draw each segment, to extend the lines at the bottom of the segment a few millimetres into the following segment so that the next person knows where to start their drawing from and the picture all joins up when it is unfolded at the end.

135. Photo Story

Prepare a story together and plan what pictures are needed to tell the story. Then create the pictures by taking photos of the group posing in the required positions (make sure you have the permission of parents/guardians for this). Print the pictures and show the story.

136. Board Game

Create a board game called 'The Master's Plan'. Let your group decide on the rules, the aim and the details of the game. There is a sample board for the game on the opposite page. Here are a couple of ideas:

- The board game could be a path that you have to move around by throwing a dice. Some squares could have directions on them. For example, 'Spend time praying, but forget what God tells you – move forward three and then back two.'

- Have a board with colours on it. Each colour represents a card that has a different type of consequence. Whatever colour you land on you have to pick up the card and do what it instructs (e.g. 'Jump five times'; 'Pray for the homeless').

Sample Board for Board Game

Grey = Take a grey activity card

White = Take a white prayer card

1	2	3	4	5	6	7
14	13	12	11	10	9	8
15	16	17	18	19	20	21
28	27	26	25	24	23	22
29	30	31	32	33	34	35
42	41	40	39	38	37	36
43	44	45	46	47	48	49

Quiz Ideas

137. Real Or Made Up?

Create a quiz of facts and fiction then get the group to decide whether the stories and events are real or made up. Tailor the questions to the age of the group. You may want to have questions relating to the Bible, current affairs, recent films, or general knowledge.

138. The Quiz

Do a general-knowledge quiz with true and false answers, but use one of the following to make it more exciting.

- If they get the answer right they take a step forward; if they get it wrong they stay still. See who can move forward the furthest during the course of the quiz.

- Choose one of the children to be the quiz leader and give them an 'answer sheet' with mostly right answers but a few wrong ones. Start with correct answers, or wrong answers for questions that are too difficult for anyone to know, but as the quiz progresses make the wrong answers more obvious. When someone questions it, allow the group to discuss it and take a vote as to what the right answer is. Encourage them that they are learning to use their own discernment and think for themselves.

139. The One Before

Split the group into pairs. One person asks questions and the other answers them. The only challenge is the person answering has to answer the question before the one they were just asked:

First person: How old are you?　　　　(Second person does not answer.)

First person: What colour is your hair?　　　Second person: 9.

First person: What do people call you at school?　　　Second person: Blonde.

140. True/False Pictures and Sounds

Hold up pictures of animals and make different animal sounds. Children have to say whether the sound is true or false (i.e. whether it matches the animal being held up).

141. Memory Game

Place 20 items on a tray (you can vary the number depending on the age of your group). Give the group two minutes to look at the items. Then remove one item without them seeing. See if they can spot the missing item. For older groups you may want to get them to write a list of everything that was on the tray, without looking at it.

142. Hangman

Split the group into two teams and play 'Hangman' against each other. One group thinks of a word and writes dashes on the board to represent each letter of the word. The other group calls out a letter one at a time. If the letter they call out is in the word then it is written into the gap(s) where it appears in the mystery word. If the letter is not in the word, then it is written up on the board and one line of a hangman's gallows is drawn. The guessing team has to guess the word before the drawing is complete. An example of the gallows is shown.

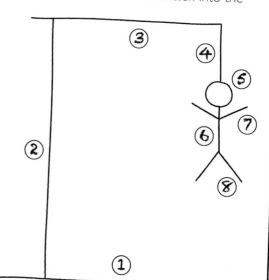

143. Who Am I?

Write the names of different people, who are either famous or known to the group, onto stickers. As each person arrives stick a sticker on their back. They must try to work out who they are by asking others questions. Questions can only be answered with a "Yes" or a "No". See how long it takes each person to guess who they are.

144. Back to School

This activity acts as a warning not to follow the crowd, or even the person who is nearly always right. It requires a small amount of preparation and briefing for two members of the group.

Pre-select two people and tell them they will be competing against each other aloud with your permission. They are not to tell the others in the group that this is a set up. One will be person 'A' and the other person 'B'.

They will be given answers to specific questions to shout out when you look in their direction after a question has been asked. When doing question nine onwards, there must not be a long delay before signalling to persons A and B. They must be able to answer the questions before the rest of the group.

Put them apart from each other but still in the circle with the rest of the group.

Now ask a series of questions and let anyone in the group respond.

Question one: $10+5=?$ (answer: 15)

Question two: $10+10=?$ (answer: 20)

Question three: $10+30=?$ (answer: 40)

Question four: $10+15-25+3-2+15=?$ (answer: 16). Person A shouts the correct answer immediately. Person B shouts, "No, that's wrong, it's 4."

Ask the rest of the group who they think is correct, or hold up a card on which is printed the correct answer (16).

Question five: $15\times2-10-20+16=?$ (answer: 16). Person A shouts the correct answer immediately. Person B shouts, "No, that's wrong, it's 10."

Ask the rest of the group who they think is correct or hold up a card on which is printed the correct answer (16).

Question six: $24\times350=?$ (answer: 8,400). Person A shouts the wrong answer immediately: 7,200. Person B replies, "No, it's 8,400."

Pretend that time is running out. Ask all who believe Person A is correct to show their hands. Then ask those who think it's B to show their hands. Note: This needs to be done quickly so the group does not get a chance to calculate the correct answer.

Show the correct answer to be 8,400.

Now discuss, by asking for responses, why they all thought that person A was correct.

Thank 'A' and 'B' and let the group know that they were part of the plan.

145. Sword Drill

The group starts with their Bibles closed and held up in the air. You call out a Bible passage (it's a good idea to write it up on a board too) and each member has to try to find it first. The first person to find it is the winner. There are lots of alternatives to Bible sword-drill games – some are given below:

Actions: The winner is the first person to find the Bible verse and do the action mentioned in the verse. Exodus 32:17 – shout; 1 Kings 18:46 – run; Mark 13:36 – sleep; Psalm 37:13 – laugh; John 11:35 – cry/weep; John 5:6 – lie down; 2 Corinthians 11:17 – talk; Ephesians 3:14 – kneel; James 5:17 – pray; Matthew 14:6 – dance.

Animals: The winner is the first person to find the verse and act like the animal in the passage. Matthew 15:27 – dog; Genesis 3:1 – serpent; Revelation 6:8 – horse; 2 Kings 2:24 – bear; Luke 8:32 – pigs; 1 Peter 2:25 – sheep; 1 Kings 13:24 – lion; Proverbs 1:17 – bird; John 12:14 – donkey; Exodus 10:4 – locust.

Colours: The winner is the first person to find the verse and then find an object in the room that is the same colour as the one mentioned in the verse. Genesis 25:25 – red; Ezekiel 27:24 – blue; Hebrews 9:4 – gold; Zechariah 6:6 – black; Psalm 51:7 – white; Leviticus 13:30 – yellow; Psalm 23:2 – green; Numbers 4:13 – purple; Isaiah 48:10 – silver; 1 Samuel 17:5 – bronze.

Jobs: The winner is the first person to act out the job mentioned in the verse. Amos 1:1 – shepherds; Leviticus 4:16 – priest; Genesis 40:16 – baker; Nehemiah 1:11 – cupbearer; Isaiah 29:16 – potter; Luke 5:2 – fishermen; Colossians 4:14 – doctor; Ezra 6:15 – king; Mark 6:3 – carpenter; 1 Kings 9:27 – sailor.

Mothers: The winner is the first person to call out the name of the mother in the verse. Genesis 3:20 – Eve; Genesis 22:20 – Milkah; Ruth 1:2 – Naomi; Ruth 4:13 – Ruth; 2 Kings 9:22 – Jezebel; 2 Timothy 1:5 – Eunice (and Lois for a bonus point!); Genesis 21:3 – Sarah; Jeremiah 31:15 – Rachel; Luke 1:57 – Elizabeth; Acts 12:12 – Mary.

Numbers: The first person to hold up the same number of fingers as the number found in the verse is the winner. Judges 18:19 – one; Revelation 9:10 – five; Hebrews 11:23 – three; Luke 19:19 – five; 1 John 5:7 – three; Galatians 1:18 – three; Luke 17:12 – ten; Acts 9:33 – eight; Revelation 11:4 – two; 2 Peter 2:5 – seven.

Objects: Place a number of objects on a table in the middle of the room. Split the group into two. Each group has to look up the reference and then send a runner to collect the object before the other group gets to it. The winner is the first team whose runner brings the object to you. Judges 14:8 – honey; Lamentations 4:4 – bread; Proverbs 27:27 – milk; 1 Samuel 17:18 – cheese; Job 31:6 – scales; Malachi 3:2 – soap; Revelation 1:18 – keys; Ruth 4:8 – sandal; Psalm 45:1 – pen; Exodus 17:12 – stone.

Parts of the body: The winner is the first person to point to the part of the body mentioned in the Bible verse. 2 Timothy 4:5 – head; Exodus 21:16 – ear; Ezekiel 8:17 – nose; John 12:38 – arm; Genesis 27:40 – neck; Ephesians 4:29 – mouth; Nehemiah 7:5 – heart; Luke 12:7 – hair; Psalm 20:8 – knees; Acts 4:35 – feet.

Welcome

146. Name Six

Go round the group and get each person to name six things in a category of your choosing. Possible categories are: places you have visited; animals you have seen; subjects you learn at school; things you like; things you don't like.

147. 60 Seconds

Divide the group into two teams. Choose a topic or an object. Have one member from the first team speak on the topic without hesitation, deviation or repetition. If they do any of these things then the other team can interrupt and stop the clock. They then present their challenge. If they are right (for example if the person repeated a word) then they score a point, someone on their team can take over and the clock continues. Whoever is speaking when 60 seconds are up gets a point for their team. A point is also given for a correct challenge, or to the other side for an incorrect challenge.

Other Games

148. I Spy

If you have a key word for the day, such as 'grace', play 'I spy' with the children but tell them that they are only allowed to spy things beginning with the same letter as the day's key word.

149. Search for Key Words

Use your Bible to find all the books in it beginning with the letters K, I, N and D. Which letter has the most books?

150. The ABC of Fruit And Veg

Get the group to get a clapping rhythm going, slapping their legs twice then clapping their hands once. The group members have to go round the room and in the time it takes to do the rhythm the first person has to say the name of a fruit or vegetable beginning with A. The next person has to say the name of a fruit or vegetable beginning with B, the person after a name beginning with C and so on. If someone can't think of a name in time they are out. This game can be simplified for younger children by slowing down the rhythm, broadening the category to anything edible, or dropping the alphabetical-order rule. Choose different categories to keep everyone on their toes.

151. Favourite Games

Encourage people to bring board games to the group one week to share with each other. It may also have to be time restricted ('Monopoly' is not the best game to play with limited time!).

152. Self-Control

Split the group into pairs. Each pair has to face each other, without laughing or smiling. When someone does they are out – reorganize the pairs and start again. If the game is going on for a long time, allow those who are out to heckle, but not touch, those who are still playing the game, to try and make them laugh.

153. Who Am I?

Play the game 'Animal, mineral or vegetable'. One person chooses an animal, a mineral or a vegetable but does not say what it is. The rest of the group is allowed to ask up to 20 questions to which the answers can only be "Yes" or "No". They have to try and find out what the person is by a process of deduction before they use up all 20 of their questions.

154. Fortunately

Sit in a circle and make up a story with each person saying one sentence in turn. The first person starts a story with the phrase, "Fortunately…". The next person goes on to say, "Unfortunately…" Then "Fortunately…", etc. E.g., "Fortunately I have lovely hair." "Unfortunately I forgot to wash it." "Fortunately I have brought shampoo in my bag."

155. Mystery

Place some mystery objects into different bags. Let the children take it in turns to put their hand in the different bags and guess what is in them. Have some simple things like a pen, as well as some yucky things – baked beans are always fun! Make sure you have cloths ready to clean hands with afterwards!

156. I Have Never

Give each person several counters – you can use toothpicks, pennies, or some similar item. The group sits in a circle and takes it in turns to say something that they have never done. For example: "I have never broken a bone," or "I have never travelled out of the country." Anyone who has done what the person has stated must give the speaker one of their counters. After going around the circle several times, the person with the most tokens wins.

157. Fast Talking

Divide the group in half and line them up in two rows. Those in one row stand back to back with those in the other row. The players standing back to back become partners. At your signal, the players turn around quickly and face their partners. They must talk to each other without stopping. They must both talk at the same time – about anything at all – and it doesn't have to make sense! All players must keep this up for 30 seconds.

You can also play this game with only two players talking at a time. They stand in the middle of the room talking fast and furiously while the others watch and laugh. A contest can be set up, with those receiving the most applause being named the winners.

158. Props

Bring various objects to the group, such as a spoon, a shoe or a specialist tool. Make them as bizarre as you like. The group has to pass round one object making up new uses for it. The only condition is that it must be something other than the use it was actually intended for. For example, a spoon could become an instrument. Or you could pretend that the shoe is the latest fashionable shape for a glass, or an ear trumpet. Have fun.

159. Catch Me

Get one person to stand behind another. The one in front should close their eyes and fall backwards without bending their knees. The person behind has to catch them. How much does the faller trust the catcher?

160. Dominoes in the Flow

Bring a set of dominoes to the group and see how long a line they can make. If you wish you can use it to show how we need to be in line with God and each other for His kingdom to work as planned.

161. Speak Out

Get the group to clap out a rhythm with their hands. Then in time to the rhythm the members of the group have to take it in turns to name something in a category you've set. Possible categories include: boy's names; girl's names; items of clothing; food; colours; animals, etc. If they cannot think of a name, take too long or repeat something already said they are out.

162. Do You Love Your Neighbour?

Get the group to stand in a circle, with one person standing in the centre. The person in the centre says to an individual in the group, "*NAME*, do you love your neighbour?" The individual asked can either reply, "Yes, I love my neighbours *NAME* and *NAME*, but I REALLY love people *(wearing green; from East London; etc.)*" or "No, I do not love my neighbours *NAME* and *NAME*."

If the person responding uses the first phrase all the members of the group with the named characteristic, plus the caller, must find a new spot in the circle at least three spaces from where they are standing. The person remaining without a space becomes the caller. If the person responding uses the second phrase, their two neighbours (those sitting directly to the left and right of them), must switch places. The second of the two to sit becomes the caller.

163. Hum That Tune

Choose four different tunes that everyone knows, such as nursery rhymes. Then give each person a piece of paper with the name of one of the four tunes on it. Each person then has to hum the tune of the song they were given and walk around until they find everyone else who is humming the same song as them, to form a group all humming their hearts out.

164. Imaginary Hide and Seek

Pick a location that everyone is familiar with, e.g. the church building. Each person needs to think of a place they could hide. Then everyone takes turns in guessing where each person is 'hiding'. (Behind a pew? Behind the bathroom door? In the wardrobe? Behind the sofa? Under the kitchen table?)

For a variation: Have the children decide what size they want to be and then pick their hiding spot. "I am the size of a mouse." This variation opens the game up to lots more imaginative hiding places.

You can also extend the potential locations to anywhere in the universe, with people asking general questions first before finding the specific location where the person is 'hiding'.

165. I'm the Most

Have all the group sit quietly and think of a superlative adjective (the 'most' something other) that describes themselves in reference to the others. They may be the youngest, the tallest, the most beautiful, or the most uptight. Then each person can share their adjective, explain it and, where possible, test its accuracy.

166. Giggle Game

Two people should face each other and without touching one another try and make the other person laugh. Whoever laughs first is out.

167. Careful!

Take a load of matches, skewers or cocktail sticks and place them randomly on top of each other on a table. The group has to take it in turns to take one away without moving any of the others. If they move one of the other sticks they are out.

168. Sing a Song

Get the group to sing a song with a difference – they have to use the words from one song with the tune from another. For example they have to sing the words of 'Baa baa black sheep' to the tune of 'Row, row, row your boat'.

169. Spot the Detail

Play a video clip or bring a detailed poster related to any subject to the group. Let the children watch it for a time and then have a quiz on some of the finer details. For example you may want to ask about the clothes somebody was wearing or what shop they walked past.

170. True or False

Get each member of the group to write down four things about themselves. Three of them should be true (the more bizarre the better). The fourth should be made up. They then read out all four 'facts' and everyone has to guess which one is the made-up one.

171. My Name

Pick a theme. It could be anything from food to cars, from animals to TV programmes.

Each person thinks up a name that becomes part of their name, which is linked to the theme. So if the theme were cars Robert could be Rolls Royce. The name does not have to start with the same letter.

Each person tells the leader their new name and the leader writes down the whole list, making sure that there are no duplicates. The leader then reads out all of the made-up names. One person is then chosen and the children have to guess which name belongs to that person.

For variation: Split the group into two teams, facing each other. One person from one group guesses the name of someone in the other team. If they get it right that person changes teams and the guesser gets to guess again. If they get it wrong then they have to join the other team. The game continues until everyone is in the same team.

172. Bible Characters

Split into groups of three or four people. Tell them that they have to stand as a freeze-frame picture depicting a Bible character. Everybody else has to guess who the character is. E.g. Daniel may be a man with lions around him. A freeze frame is like an acted scene, but nobody is allowed to move (it's a photo instead of a film).

173. Silly Welcome

Get the group to welcome each other in the silliest way possible, but they are not allowed to laugh!

174. Shopping Trip

Sit in a circle. The first person says, "I went shopping and I bought a ...." The next person has to say both the item they bought and the item that the previous person bought. The next person repeats the previous two items and adds their own, and so on.

For example:

Person one: I went shopping and I bought a shark.

Person two: I went shopping and I bought a shark and a hat.

Person three: I went shopping and I bought a shark, a hat and a banana-split ice cream.

If they miss anything out then they are out.

Other Ideas

175. Video Slot

Have an age-appropriate,
fun Christian video ready and play a section
for ten minutes to welcome the children in.

176. Let's be Nice

Give each child a piece of paper and a
pen. Ask them to write down the names of those in the
group (if the group is very large split it into two). They
should leave space between each name. Then get them to
write something nice about that group member in the
space. Imagine having ten children all saying ten positive
things to one person in a couple of minutes – this is more
than some of them get in a month.

177. Prepare the Way

Get the group to prepare the meeting
room for the King. How would they want the place
to look when God comes? Raise their expectations
that they will be meeting with God in the group
time today.

178. Goals for the Year

Get the group to think about what they want to do in
the next 12 months. Give each group member a small
notebook. They can decorate the front cover and, on the
first page, write their goals down. They can then use the
rest of the book as a prayer diary for the year, recording
what God says to them.

179. Airmail

Get each person to
write a note to someone in the room.
They should then turn the note into a
paper aeroplane and send it to that
person by 'airmail'.

Welcome

180. Culture Day

Hold a culture day where you celebrate a country's culture with its clothes, food, photos, etc.

181. Joke Time

Go round the group and let each person tell a joke that they know.

182. Unique

Have fun showing the unique things you can do, and challenging each other to do impossible things. To get everyone started here are a few: Can you lick your elbow? Can you touch your nose with your tongue? Can you turn your tongue upside down?

Worship

Contents

Introduction

Worship is more than singing songs to God. We can worship God without singing and we can sing songs without worshipping. The essence of this time is to connect with Daddy God's heart in worship.

Of course this is not something that we can make those under our care do, rather it is something that they have to choose for themselves. They can conform outwardly to everything we ask of them, but without connecting with God in their hearts. Our role is simply to provide the forum in which it is as easy as possible for them to worship the Lord.

More important than any of the activity ideas in this section, if we are to lead the group into worship, is the need to be worshippers ourselves. This is not something that we can fake, but as we spend time worshipping God at home on our own, it will overflow into our leading on a Sunday.

Worshipping hearts inspire others to worship.

As you are using the activity ideas, remember the key purpose is to allow each person to connect with God in worship. Let this provide the focus for the ways in which you lead the group each week as they come to worship God.

Visual Worship

183. Visual Praise

Bring, or ask group members
to bring, Christian music videos to the group. This
can be used to aid the worship. Make sure you
select some songs they are familiar with and
encourage them not to watch others worshipping
but to worship God for themselves.

184. Light It Up

Get the group to bring
torches or other lights, such as mobile phones, to
the meeting. Use the lights to worship God – be
creative. You've probably heard of a wave offering,
why not have a light offering!

185. Restore the Meaning of Christmas

Using Christmas decorations or other Christmassy objects get the
group to worship Jesus. For example you may want to give them
Christmas decorations which they can then wave to God as you
sing a song, or they can get dressed up in tinsel in preparation for a
special time of worship.

186. Laying Crowns before God

The book of Revelation speaks of how rulers will
lay their crowns before God as a way of saying
that although they are monarchs, they submit to
God's rule. Get the group to sing and worship
God with crowns on their heads. They can then
take the crowns off and give them to God as they
bow before Him.

187. Worth-ship

Worship means that we give
to something what it is worth (Worth-ship) –
what it deserves. When it comes to worshipping
God He is worthy of everything we have. Bring
out various objects and get the group to think
about how they can give God worship – let this
lead into a time of worship. Objects may include
money, clothes and toys.

188. All Creation

God made the whole world.
Get your group to make a large picture of the world together as an act of worship to God.

189. Approach the Throne Room

Build a throne in the middle of the room. Tell the group that you can't just go up to a king whenever you feel like it; think about what could happen if you did. But with God as King, we can go whenever we want to, because He is our Father. Encourage the group to approach God's throne, worshipping Him as He deserves.

190. Worship Dream

Get the group to close their eyes and imagine that they are standing in front of their whole school to lead worship. How would they encourage everyone to do it? Get them to act as if they are leading their whole school in worship (for example by asking them to lift their hands and sing to God).

191. Act It

Take an action song that your group enjoys. Sing it a couple of times. Then get the group to 'sing' it using the actions only. They can then also sing it with the words only.

192. The Holy of Holies

Using a map of the tabernacle, plot out different areas in your room. Have the group move through the different parts of the tabernacle until they end with the holy of holies. They start in the outer courts, then pass into the holy place then on into the holy of holies, where before Jesus' death only the high priest was allowed, and then only once a year. As they go through each stage encourage them to become more intimate in their worship.

193. Worship En Masse

Play a video of worship from a large conference. Get the group to imagine they are part of the conference and join in the worship.

194. Railway Worship

Draw out two lines of rails and give each person pieces of paper that will act as railway sleepers to join the rails. On the paper they should write a worship thought or draw a worship picture. As they finish each one, add it to the railway track to make the track longer. When everyone has added all their thoughts walk along it like a train, encouraging them to express the different thoughts to God as they pass over each sleeper.

195. Choose A Colour

Bring sweets or tags of different colours to the group. Let the group members choose one from a bag. The colour they choose will decide the style of worship. For example: Red=Praise, Black=Silent, Yellow=Worship, Blue=Rap. The group could help decide what each colour stands for as a way of exploring different forms of worship.

196. Wave Offering

Bring tree branches to the group and use them to wave to God, just like people did to Jesus when He entered Jerusalem.

197. Leader's Mantle

Bring a hat to the group. Whoever is wearing the hat is the worship leader. After a few minutes they must pass the hat on to someone else. Encourage them not simply to pass on the hat to anyone, but to see who they feel God wants to lead the worship next.

198. WORSHIP Acronym

Write down the word 'worship' and get the group in teams or on their own to think of sentences that express worship to God, one for each letter in the word 'worship'. For example:

Worthy are you, Lord.

Only you are God.

Radiant in all your ways.

Sing to you.

Holy is your name.

Indescribable are your works.

Praise to you.

199. Write A Song

Get the group to work together to write a song. Start with the lyrics. Ask the group what aspect of God they want to worship. Help them to develop it from there. Add music, rhythm, and even actions or a dance as appropriate. When you have completed it get the group to perform it to the Lord.

Creative Worship

200. Nursery-rhyme Worship

Get the group to make up new words to the nursery rhymes they know. Their new words should be worship to God. The whole group can then join in the worship.

201. Cross Centred

Get the group to listen to a song about Jesus on the cross and to think about His death. After this they can write a love letter to Jesus (or draw Him a picture) to say thanks for all that He has done.

202. Banners

Make banners or streamers for God and use them to worship Him.

203. Rap Liturgy

Take some set words, for example liturgy from the Anglican Church, and turn them into a rap. (For example: The Lord is here – His Spirit is with us. Lift up your hearts – we lift them to the Lord. Let us give thanks to the Lord our God – it is right to give Him thanks and praise.)

204. Dance before the Lord

Get the group, either as a whole or in smaller groups, to make up a dance to a praise song. Play the track as they prepare the dance then let them use the dance to worship God.

Worship

205. Coloured Flags

Bring to group material of
different colours that can be used as flags. Each colour should represent a style of worship – shouting praise, thanksgiving, singing, etc. As you (or a chosen member of the group) wave a flag, the rest of the group can start to worship God in the way that corresponds to the colour of the flag.

206. An Imaginary Band for Real Worship

Form an imaginary band to worship God. The band could be made up of imaginary instruments, or instruments made out of everyday objects such as elastic bands for twanging and tables for beating rhythms.

207. Thank God

Let each person write
God a thank-you note or card.

208. Learn A New Song

Is your group ready for some fresh worship? This could be a good time to introduce some new songs.

209. The Modern Book of Psalms

Explain to the group how the book of Psalms is full of praise poems to God. Some of them are sorry songs, others are praise, others are cries for help (you may want to show examples of these). Ask each person in the group to write different poems of praise to God.

210. Modern Hymn

The words of traditional
hymns are fantastic expressions of worship. Get the group to update a hymn, perhaps by turning it into a rap or having a strong rhythm going on in the background.

211. Psalm It!

Choose a psalm before the meeting and print a copy of the words for each person. Then let them make up a tune and/or actions to go with the words. Learn the psalm and use it in praise to God. Possible psalms include: 1, 8, 23, 24, 29, 47, 48, 66, 75, 117, 121, 149, 150.

212. The Nature of God

Create a picture, as a group, in an act of worship to God. The theme of the picture could be the nature of God (or for younger children – what God is like!). Use pictures and words, and be creative in your worship as a group.

213. Colour Praise

Bring sheets or ribbon of different colours to the group. Ask the group what the colours represent then use the ribbons to make a dance to the Lord. Examples of what the colours could mean: White=God is Holy; Red=Blood of Jesus, etc.

214. Play Back

Create a rap or a song and record it on your phone to use in future worship times.

215. Worship Letter

Get the group to write a letter to God telling Him how wonderful He is.

216. Worship Tree

Draw a tree on a large sheet of paper before the group begins. Then during the worship time let each person hang an expression of their worship to God on the tree.

Worship

217. A New Song

Work together as a group to write a new song. Choose a well-known tune and let the group create alternative words, to God. For example, they could take the tune from 'We wish you a merry Christmas' and change the words to 'I'm living just for Jesus, I'm living just for Jesus, I'm living just for Jesus, and I love Him so much'.

218. Sing Out

Start by leading the children to worship God. Then when they are worshipping encourage them to make up a song to God on the spot and sing it out loud. This will require them to take a step of faith, but it will be an awesome worship experience for them as they do it.

219. Declaration of Worship

Work together to write a declaration of worship to God then say it together.

Non-singing Worship

220. He's Coming Soon

Get the group members to see what a difference it will make when Jesus returns. Encourage them to ask Him to return. Play some suitable music of Jesus' return in the background as they do this.

221. Worship Through Service

Get the group to think of things they can do as an act of worship to God. For example they could help their mum at home. Get them to dedicate these actions to God as an act of worship and follow up on their worship next week.

222. Thank You, Jesus

Get the members of the group to think about their day one bit at a time. For each part of the day encourage them to think of something to thank God for.

223. Noisy Praise

Get the group to make as much noise as they possibly can to praise God. To build up to it, tell the group that at a football match people make lots of noise because they are excited about the match. How much more noise should we make, as we are excited about Jesus and what He has done for us? Make sure that the focus of the worship time stays on Jesus.

224. Shout It Out

Listen to God carefully for 30 seconds. Think about all God has done. Then take 30 seconds to shout out praise to God. Switch between being silent and shouting several times.

Worship

225. Silent Praise

Tell the group that they have to praise God in different ways from their heart – but they are not allowed to make any noise as they do it!

226. Share A Testimony

Get the group to share good things God has done for them so far this year. This is a form of worship as we give God worth, acknowledging that He is at work in our lives. As each person shares, everyone else can shout praise to God for what He has done.

227. Only Worship

Get the group to stand in a circle. Let one person start by worshipping God out loud with a prayer. They should keep doing this until they stop worshipping and start asking God for something (e.g. "Father you are so wonderful, please be with us here now"). As soon as they ask for anything blow a whistle and the next person in the circle can start to worship God.

228. Worship in Truth

Get the group to work on a list of the top ten greatest things about God. When they have made the list get them to shout it, or chant it, to God together.

229. No Voice, No Instruments

If you had no instruments and no voice how could you worship God? Encourage your group to do this. Then let them worship God with their voices too.

230. Worship Service

Explain to the group that our obedience to God is a way of worshipping Him. Get the group to think of ways to serve each other as an act of worship, and then they can do it. For example they may serve each other a drink, pray for each other, help each other with a problem, or make a card for each other.

231. Clean Feet

Explain to the group that this week you are going to demonstrate a way that we can worship God. Wash the feet of those in your group and as you do so tell them what Jesus did and explain why He did it.

232. Worship in Action

Explain to the group that each person is special to God. God made everybody! Get the group to think about each other and then respond to God with a sentence starting "God, it's amazing the way that you made *NAME* to …"

233. Past Worship

Get the group to look back at the past week and think of ways in which they have worshipped God. When they have thought of the ways, bring them before the Lord to tell Him how these were their expressions of worship through the week.

234. Think about the Cross

Bring a cross (or make one) and get the children to look at it. As they look at it tell them why Jesus died on the cross. As you tell them let them kneel before Jesus and thank Him for dying for them.

235. Chant

Get the group to repeat a chant to God after you, or after a member of the group.

236. Worship Tunnel

Bring several toilet-roll tubes to the group. Then get each person to speak praise to God into the cardboard tube before passing it on to someone else.

237. With the Angels

The angels worship God all the time. Get the group to worship God with the angels. Start off quietly and gradually get louder and louder, using phrases such as "Holy, holy, holy," from Revelation 4:8.

238. Worship Blanket

Bring a blanket to the group. Let each member of the group hold on to a piece of the blanket. Then as the whole group throws the blanket up into the air let them shout out their praises to God. Repeat this several times.

239. Bible Declaration

Take a passage of Scripture that is worshipful and declare it together as a group, in worship to God.

240. Tithes and Offerings

Encourage the group to bring their tithes and offerings each week, as an act of worship to God. Collect the offering, and thank God that we have something to give Him.

241. It Would Have Been Enough

Work together to build up the story of all the things that God has done for all of us, in the order of the events that have happened. After the list has been completed, put it all together as follows: "God, if you had only …that would have been enough." For example: "God, if you had only decided to make us that would have been enough." "God, if you had only made us and given us food that would have been enough." Build this up and then at the end celebrate everything that God has done for us. End with a loud shout of praise.

242. Stadium Chant

Get the group to imagine they are in a football stadium, preparing to worship Jesus. What chants would they call out to Him? When they have made up some chants get them to chant them together to God.

243. Alphabet Worship

Calling out one letter of the alphabet at a time, get each member of the group to shout out as many words as they can think of beginning with that letter which describe God.

A – Awesome, Available; B – Big; C – Creator, Caring, etc.

244. Worship in Truth

Give everyone party poppers and whistles. Take it in turns to thank God for something that He has done for us. Tell the others if they agree with the thing the person has just said, they should use their party instruments to thank God as loudly as they can.

Worship

245. Communion

Take Communion as a group.
If you want to why not have a meal with it and make it a special event as you share together, remembering what Jesus did on the cross.

246. The Gospel Story Praise

Tell the Good News of all that God has done. As you share each thing let everyone shout out "GOD IS GOOD". They may have their own things that they want to share.

For example:

God made us. GOD IS GOOD.

God loves us. GOD IS GOOD.

God sent Jesus. GOD IS GOOD.

Jesus died on the cross for us. GOD IS GOOD.

Jesus takes away our sins. GOD IS GOOD.

The Holy Spirit is here to help us. GOD IS GOOD.

God showed us Himself. GOD IS GOOD.

247. Ten Commandments Worship

Use each of the Ten Commandments to lead into worship for God. Give a 20-second intro. for each commandment and then allow 40 seconds of worshipping God.

For example:

Do not steal – we should not steal worship from God.

Do not lie – we should worship God in spirit and in truth.

Do not murder – let God live in our hearts.

Honour your father and mother – God is our Father, we should honour Him.

248. Stars

Give each child some stars, and
get them to write on them things that God has
done for them. Then take each of the stars and wave
them before God for everything He has done.

249. The Names of God

Write down some of the names of God. Call out one
name at a time and get the group to speak out worship to God for that
aspect of His character.

1. Jehovah-Elohim – the Eternal Creator (Genesis 2:4-25)

2. Adonai-Jehovah – the Lord our Sovereign; Master Jehovah (Genesis 15:2, 8)

3. Jehovah-Jireh – the Lord will see or provide (Genesis 22:8-14)

4. Jehovah-Nissi – the Lord our Banner (Exodus 17:15)

5. Jehovah-Rapha – the Lord our Healer (Exodus 15:26)

6. Jehovah-Shalom – the Lord our Peace (Judges 6:24)

7. Jehovah-Tsidqenuw – the Lord our Righteousness (Jeremiah 23:6; 33:16)

8. Jehovah-Mekaddishkem – the Lord our Sanctifier (Exodus 31:13; Leviticus 20:8; 21:8; 22:9, 16, 32; Ezekiel 20:12)

9. Jehovah-Sabaoth – the Lord of hosts (1 Samuel 1:3; etc., 284 times)

10. Jehovah-Shammah – the Lord is present (Ezekiel 48:35)

11. Jehovah-Elyown – the Lord Most High (Psalm 7:17; 47:2, 97:9)

12. Jehovah-Rohi – the Lord my Shepherd (Psalm 23:1)

13. Jehovah-Hoseenu – the Lord our Maker (Psalm 95:6)

14. Jehovah-Eloheenu – the Lord our God (Psalm 99:5, 8, 9)

15. Jehovah-Eloheka – the Lord your God (Exodus 20:2, 5, 7)

16. Jehovah-Elohay – the Lord my God (Zechariah 14:5)

Active Worship

250. Foot Worship

Encourage the group to use their feet in worship – they could dance or play instruments with their feet. Highlight how we should worship God by what we do wherever we go.

251. Praise Him! Praise Him!

Bring to the group a variety of spoons. These could include wooden spoons, plastic spoons, metal spoons, small ones and big ones. Ensure they are all appropriate for the age group. You will also need some vibrant praise music. Encourage the group to use the spoons as instruments to play along with the music. As they are doing this remind them to keep their focus on our awesome God. Let there be joy in God's presence.

252. The Worship Whistle

Tell the group that they have to worship God for something He has done. Every time you blow a whistle (or clap your hands) they have to move around the room. When you blow the whistle again they should stand still and worship God for something different. Explain they can worship God with their words or with a song, or by any other creative means.

253. Worship Lifestyle

Set an alarm to go off in the group every five minutes. Tell the group that whenever they hear the alarm they have to get to their feet and praise God. At the end of group explain that we should worship God all the time.

254. Worship Skips

Have two children hold a skipping rope while another one skips. The rest of the group has to sing or chant a worship song. When the person in the middle falters, someone else takes over skipping.

Worship

255. Distracted?

Split the group into two. One half worships God and the other half tries to distract them. Encourage the worshippers to keep on worshipping God from their hearts despite the distractions. The distracters can do whatever they want but must not touch the worshippers. Swap over so everyone has an opportunity to worship.

256. Celebratory Chant

Lead the group in a celebratory chant for God. Bring some mini flags that they can wave as they chant out praise to Him.

257. The Can-Can

Form a line and do a can-can-style dance, or move as a train, as you worship God together.

258. Zones

Create different zones around the room where the group can go to worship God in different ways. You may want to have zones for thanks, praise, worship, listening, etc. Mark each zone with a sign so the children can remember what they should do in each area.

259. Climb the Ladder

Climb the worship ladder: Start with thanks, then move on to praise, then worship, then meditation on God, then listening to Him. You may want to draw out the worship ladder on the floor for the group to climb. As they go through the different stages encourage them in their worship by speaking words that keep their focus on God.

260. Postures

We can worship God in all sorts of ways. Sometimes people stand; others sit, kneel or even lie down before God. Get the group to worship God in each of these positions and then tell you how it affected their worship. Then allow them to worship God in whatever position they would like to.

261. Clap-A-Thon

Clap and cheer to God as loud as you can for as long as you can – He's worth it!

262. Shepherds and Wise Men

Discuss how the shepherds and wise men worshipped Jesus. For example, they brought Him gifts, they came see Him, and they bowed down to Him. Encourage your group to do the same as you worship God together.

263. A Worship Wave

Get the group to sit in a line and do a Mexican wave, standing up in turn and lifting their hands. As they do this they should shout "Hallelujah" as loudly as they can in worship to God. When you have practised it a couple of times encourage them, as they shout, really to shout out to God.

264. Worship March

Get the children to march around for God, singing a worship song as they do so. For younger groups you may want to provide musical instruments for them to play as they do this. For older groups you may want to march on the spot as a form of warfare mixed with worship.

265. Instrumental Praise

Read Psalm 150 to the group and then give out all kinds of instruments for them to use as the psalmist suggests. They could even use table tops and hands as drums, and bunches of keys as shakers.

266. Group Worship

Divide the group into two and get each group to sing different sections of a song. This works best for songs which can easily be divided up into alternate lines, such as 'Hallelu, hallelu, hallelu, hallelujah'. When they sing their part they should stand up; when they are not singing they must sit back down again.

267. Worship at All Times

Explain to the group that we should worship God in all circumstances. Get them to think of a situation where they should worship God, then worship God together imagining you are in that situation. Then get them to suggest another situation. Move to a different part of the room to worship God together in that new situation. Continue this until the time is up – remember that we should worship God in the bad times as well as the good ones!

Child-led Worship

268. Look What the Lord Has Done

Get people to share a song that is important to them, and ask them to explain why. They can then choose whether to sing it as a solo testimony, or have the rest of the group join in with them.

269. Solo Items

Allow one or two people to sing a song, or do something else to worship God. Make sure you give them advance warning so that they have time to pray and prepare and follow up with them to check how their prayers and preparation are going. The others in the group can listen, and worship God in their hearts. Remind those up front that they are not there to perform to the group but to worship God.

270. My Favourite Song

Get each person to share what their favourite worship song is. Ask them to say why they like it and then sing it together as a group.

271. Karaoke Worship

Using videos and setting up a microphone (if you can – if not, have a pretend microphone to hand) invite different members of the group to lead the group in worship with different songs, karaoke style.

272. Spirit Led

Wait for God to prompt somebody in the group to lead worship. Explain that if they think of a worship song they can lead everyone else to sing it. If no one has anything to say just sit in silence waiting on God to speak to someone.

273. New Songs

Learn five new worship
songs then discuss which one the group like the
most and why. Use this song to worship God.

274. Boys vs. Girls

Let the group worship God, with boys
and girls taking it in turns to worship Him.

275. You Lead

Let the group take it in turns
to lead all the members into worship.
Warn them in advance so that they
have time to prepare.

Musical Worship

276. Praise from Every Nation

We are now blessed with great Christian worship from around the world. Collect some samples from as many continents as possible and play them to the group. Encourage everyone to praise God in some small way as they experience the music of our other brothers and sisters in Christ.

277. Instrumental Worship

Get the group to build up a beat to the Lord. They may do this by clapping their hands, tapping a table, jangling keys, or even using percussion instruments. Some group members may want to make up a rap to God to this rhythm. In it all keep the focus on making music for the Lord.

278. Worship Bonanza

Hold a worship bonanza for an extended time in the group, encouraging the group to remember that at the heart of discipleship is Jesus, and He is the one we worship.

279. Rap It

Choose a song with which to rap to God.

280. Up to Zion

Focus your worship this week on the nation of Israel. You can do this by bringing music to the group that expresses God's passion for the nation of Israel, His promises for His chosen people, and so on. Simply play the music to the group and ask how they appreciate this compared with what they usually use.

Worship

281. Meditate on God

Play a quieter worship song and have the group sit quietly and think about God, then let them tell Him their thoughts. They could simply speak out their thoughts to Him, or they could draw, or write, their response.

282. Carols in Worship

Sing some Christmas carols to worship God. Why not even get the group to go door to door singing carols and sharing tracts (this could tie in with the witness activity for the week)? Ensure that you get the permission of parents/guardians and that you have enough adults for the group if you choose to do this.

283. Music of the Moment

Get the group to bring in Christian tracks that they listen to and play the tracks for all to hear.

284. Soak in God

Explain to the group that you are just going to sit in God's presence. Play a worshipful track in the background as the group sits before God. Encourage them not to be distracted and to keep their focus on God. Move around the room praying for each one of them really to encounter God as they do this.

285. Worship into His Presence

Using worship songs, perhaps on a track, lead the group into God's presence to worship Him intimately. Don't settle for them just singing the songs, but encourage them to sing from their hearts to Him.

286. Recorded Worship

Explain to the group how God keeps a record of our worship and prayers to Him. Revelation tells us that He collects the prayers of the saints in a bowl. Tell the group that you are going to record their worship today and that they should worship from the bottom of their hearts so that there will be a record of how much they love God in the future. Use a mobile phone or a video camera to record their worship (remember to check with parents/guardians before filming the children).

287. Devoted

Choose a devotional song to sing to God. As the children are worshipping encourage them to kneel before God, close their eyes and lift their hands to Him if they want to give Him everything.

288. No Barriers

Get the group to close their eyes and worship God with all their hearts. Put on a music track and encourage them not to worry about what others think, but simply to worship God with all their heart.

289. Worship Band

Create a band by encouraging the group to bring instruments they can play. Worship God together. Those who do not play an instrument can play percussion or be backing singers. Encourage them not just to play the instrument, but to worship God in their heart as they play.

290. Eyes Closed

Tell the group that you are going to worship God for 10 minutes, and that during that time they are not allowed to open their eyes, so that they will not be distracted. Then lead them in worshipping God, encouraging them to worship Him from their hearts.

291. Worship Him

Take a psalm of praise and use this as the basis for worship. Get someone to read the psalm out loud and, as it is read, everyone else should do what it says, such as "make a joyful noise".

292. Worship Sandwich

Get the group to enter into God's presence through worship. When they are there encourage them to listen to what God says. They can then respond with worship.

293. Think Then Worship

Get the group to think about all God has done for them before they start to worship. After a time of sitting in silence, lead them to worship the Lord.

Worship

Worship

294. DVD

Bring a worship
DVD to group. Pump up the volume
and let the group get lost in worship.

295. Volume Level

Start by showing your group a volume
indicator (this may be a long piece of paper with a blob of
Blu-Tack which can be moved up and down it, or more simply
you can just use your hand). Tell them that when the indicator is
at the top they should sing at the top of their voices, but when
it is down at the bottom they should be as quiet as possible. Let
them start worshipping and adjust the volume as you worship.

296. Don't Worship

Choose a worship song. Then get the
group to sing it. Once they have sung it once, tell them
that you want them to sing the song, but they are *not
allowed* to worship God – they can only sing it. Then tell
them they should sing the song again, but this time they
should worship God with all their heart as they sing it.

297. Songs that Teach

Choose songs that teach biblical
truths – perhaps even a hymn!

298. Intercontinental

Choose music and styles of worship
from different continents and let the group worship as
they do in different parts of the world.

299. Beat Box

Let the group members take
it in turns to provide a beat box as
everyone else worships God in song
with their voices.

Other

300. The God of Abraham, Isaac and Jacob

Get the group to worship different aspects of God, as demonstrated by the lives of Abraham, Isaac and Jacob:

The God of Abraham spoke destiny.

The God of Isaac spoke joy.

The God of Jacob spoke fruitfulness and fulfilment.

301. From God's Point of View

Get the group to worship God. Stop periodically to ask them what God thinks about their worship. Use this to encourage them to worship God even more.

302. Prepare the Way

As you come to worship God encourage the group to start with a time of repentance and then to sing worship to God. Finally allow the Holy Spirit to minister to each child individually, praying for them as led by the Holy Spirit.

303. Intercessory Worship

Discuss an area of life where it looks like God is not Lord. Then bring that area to God and worship Him while thinking of this area. This is declaring Him to be God even if it does not look like it – it is giving God the dominion over this area.

304. 101 Reasons

As a group over a few weeks think of 101 reasons why we should worship God. As the children think of each thing, pause to worship God for that reason for a few moments. This should be a fast-moving worship time, so encourage your group to engage quickly.

Worship

305. Candles

Light some candles around the room
(be aware of safety issues here). God is our light. Get the
group to look at the candles; they have a mystical simplicity
about them that is transfixing – you can look at them for a
long time. God desires that we gaze at Him in the same way.

306. Whatever the Weather

Make some pictures of different types of weather: the sun, clouds, etc.
Explain that these pictures show how we may feel on the inside at
times. But no matter how we feel we should worship God. Start to
worship God and display the different weather pictures. The children
should follow the feelings of the pictures, but still keep worshipping
God throughout the time.

307. Prophetic Worship

Lead the group in a time of prophetic
worship – listening to God and worshipping Him
as He leads, responding to words that He gives.

308. Praise

Read passages of Scripture from the Old
Testament and then read their fulfilment in the
New Testament. Praise God for His Word fulfilled.

309. Instruments

Make instruments and
use them in worship to God.

310. Harmonize

Sing a song in harmony for
God's glory.

311. An Order

God deserves and demands
praise from us. No matter how we feel,
God deserves our praise. Encourage
the group to worship God from the
bottom of their hearts.

312. Worship Commitment

Discuss how people worship TV, their computer or even their mobile phone. Call the children to make a commitment during this session to worship only God, for real, from their hearts.

313. Remember It!

Learn Psalm 23 together as a group to use in worship.

314. The Heavens Declare

Psalm 19:1 says the heavens declare the glory of God. Think together as a group about how they do this. Then join with the heavens to declare God's glory. If possible go outside to worship God under the open heavens.

315. Love God

Encourage the group to think about their love of God before they start to worship Him and then to worship Him out of their love for Him.

316. Hard Times

Get the group to think about hard times in the last year. Encourage them to worship God because He is in control. In other words, encourage them to turn a '?' into a '!' – to turn a 'Why is this happening?' into a 'God is faithful!'

317. Pour Out Your Heart

Encourage the group to pour out their hearts to God as they worship Him. They can think about all that He has done for them and about who He is. Lead them from this reflection to respond to Him, being real about what is really going on inside them.

Worship

Word

Contents

Introduction

In this section there are a number of creative ideas that will help enhance your teaching of the Bible. As part of a healthy diet it is not enough for the children and young people simply to have the food on the plate – they need to eat it, digest it and be affected by it.

To help with this process of digestion it is good to choose a **Take-home Key** – something that the children should remember. To help them live out the Word you serve each week, you can also give an **Action Point** – something for them to actually do in the coming week.

Real value from your teaching will come not just when you give a take-home key and an action point, but when your group actually remember what you taught and do what you have told them to do. So having set the challenge, make sure you set aside time in the meeting the week after to follow up on these two points to see if they can still remember the take-home key and how they got on with implementing the action point.

This reinforcement of teaching is vital if the children are going to grow with God. We want them to live out God's Word in their lives, not just to learn about it. Just as we encourage children to eat their vegetables, because we know it is good for them, so we can encourage them to live for God during the week, because we know that His way leads to life.

Word

In-depth Study

318. Not Fully Right

Read through the passage for the week and ask the group, "If this was the only part of the Bible that we had access to, what would we get right, and what would we get wrong, compared with what we know from the rest of the Bible?" To put it another way, what would be the gaps in our understanding, or what would we be in danger of misunderstanding? Explain that we need to know the whole Bible if we want to be able to grasp individual passages fully. This is one reason why we should read the Bible daily.

319. Bible-study Rap

This activity can either be done as a whole group or individually. Use the following rap to help your group study the Bible:

"What? Who? Why? Apply it to today."

Start by chanting the Bible-study rap above, before leading the group through each of the steps in the rap.

What?: Think of as many questions as you can, relating to the Bible passage, that begin with the word **'What'**. Try to answer each of these questions and then ask any more questions that the answers bring to mind. Answer these follow-on questions and ask any more questions that the answers bring to mind. Carry on doing this until you run out of questions.

Who?: When you have finished with the 'What' questions move on to think of as many questions as you can, relating to the Bible passage, that start with **'Who'**. Answer the 'Who' questions and ask any more questions that the answers bring to mind. Continue this process until you run out of questions.

Why?: When you have finished with the 'Who' questions move on to think of as many questions as you can, relating to the Bible passage, that start with **'Why'**. Answer the 'Why' questions and any follow-on questions until you run out of questions.

Apply it to today: Finally, think about how you can **apply** what you have learnt **to** your life **today**. This may provide an action point for the week.

320. Two Questions

Before you meet with your group, study the Bible passage carefully (you may want to use the Bible-study rap to help you). As a result of your in-depth study, think of two questions where the discussion of these questions will provide a detailed understanding of the passage. Then ask these two questions in the group.

321. For Further Study

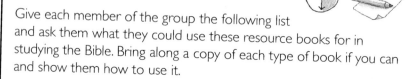

Give each member of the group the following list and ask them what they could use these resource books for in studying the Bible. Bring along a copy of each type of book if you can and show them how to use it.

- Bible dictionary (we recommend *The Baker Bible Dictionary* for kids)
- Concordance
- Commentary
- Bible maps
- Lexicon (E.g. Strong's Lexicon)

All these book types can be found for free on the internet.

322. Private Investigation

Look at each person mentioned in the passage. Act as private investigators to compile a report giving as much information on each person as possible.

323. What Can We Learn about God?

Explain that the Bible is there to help us understand more about God and our relationship to Him. Therefore we can read any Bible passage and ask ourselves this question: "What do we learn about God?"

324. Meditate on It

Choose a very small passage (one verse is best) and get the group to keep thinking about this one verse for five to ten minutes in silence, to see what they can learn. Help them to remain focused on the task by reading the passage out loud during the time of silence. Talk about this time afterwards.

Word

325. What Style?

Talk about the style of the passage you are reading. It may be history, poetry, a speech or even a letter. Having established the style, talk about what things the group would expect to find in this genre of writing. Then see how many of these things you can find in today's passage. For example in a letter you would expect an address, who it was to and who it was from. In history you would expect key facts and perhaps the writer's own bias. Poetry is often full of emotions.

326. Colour the Passage

Give everyone a photocopy of the Bible passage and some coloured pencils or pens. Ask them to underline words that are repeated in this passage, using a different colour for each word. Next, ask them to put a coloured circle around words that have the same kind of idea or meaning, again using a different colour for each idea (e.g. 'die' and 'died' would be one colour).

This exercise will take quite a while, but is worth the time. For younger groups you can play it as more of a game all together – spotting the words that are the same – and together you can underline the words as they find them. By the end of it all the passage will look very colourful. Some colours will be found throughout the passage, others in only one section. These colours will help you to work out more about what the passage is saying. Discuss what jumps out from the passage and think about what this may mean.

327. Who Were You?

Bring Bible dictionaries, internet pages and any other resources you can find, to help the group discover more about the people in the Bible. Think about who they were, where they came from, how they might have travelled, and the significance of their life as shown in today's passage.

328. Tested

Tell the group what passage of the Bible you will be studying next week and ask them to read it during the week. Then warn them that you are going to start the following week by testing them on the passage. That week, prepare a list of questions on the passage to find out how well they have read it. You may want to give them time during the session to revise. The difficulty of the test will depend on their age, but ask a mix of easy questions and ones that will require them to have read the passage carefully. Explain that it is important that we read the Bible carefully if we are to learn what God is saying.

Word

329. The Context

Discuss the context of the passage that you are studying together: Who wrote it? Who did they write it for? Why did they write it? What do the passages either side of this passage say? What does this tell us about what the author wanted us to understand from this passage? After all a text without a context can become a pretext for whatever you want it to say, so it is important that we don't just look at a verse in isolation from its surroundings.

330. Timeline

Bring a Bible timeline to the group.
Show them where this week's passage sits on the timeline.

331. Define It

Take some key words from the passage and ask people to explain what the words mean. Discuss how thinking about the meaning of individual words can help us understand the passage as a whole.

Word

332. The Gospel in Everything

At the core of the Bible is the Gospel of grace. In nearly every passage of the Bible you can find a signpost to God's grace. Challenge the group from time to time to find the link.

Thinking About the Story

333. A Puzzle

Show your group just one piece from a puzzle. Ask them to work out what picture the whole puzzle will form. Then gradually give them the rest of the pieces, so they can put the puzzle together. Go on to explain how each part of the Bible is a part of the whole. Talk about today's passage and how it fits into the bigger picture. We need the whole Bible to understand fully each part. As we read through the whole Bible regularly we gradually build up the full picture of what God is saying. Go round the group to find out whether each person is reading the Bible at home each day, and if so find out how much they are reading. Older ones can read a chapter a day; younger ones can use Bible study notes to guide their reading.

Word

334. Reporter

Get your group to write newspaper articles on the day's story. They will need to think carefully of the main headline as this will tell people what the key message of the story is. If they are too young to write, they can draw a picture of the key events.

335. Get Ready

Get the group to think about how they have to prepare for different things. They can either talk about it, or act it out. Possible scenarios include preparing for exams, preparing to go camping, or preparing to go to school. Bring some props with you to illustrate these different things. Talk about how God prepared the character in the story for the events in the passage you are studying today.

336. Family Tree

Draw out your family tree on a piece of paper. Ask everyone else to do the same, putting in as many people as they know. Then draw out the family tree of the characters in the Bible story, to help the group understand how the whole Bible fits together and how this passage fits into the bigger picture.

337. Over the Top

Read the Bible passage out loud, using over-the-top expressions and emotions. Make it as theatrical as possible! Then discuss together what the different people involved in the story must have been feeling.

338. With Life

Read the story in the most dramatic way possible, varying your tone and volume to engage the children as much as possible.

339. The Professor Explains

After you have read the story get one person to act as 'Professor' and explain in one minute what it was all about.

340. Feeding Time

If your Bible passage mentions food, bring some along for everyone to share, (although if you are studying John the Baptist you may want to leave the locusts at home on this occasion!). Remember to check for allergies and intolerances first.

341. Photo Shoot

Using a digital camera, build up a series of shots for a modern re-enactment of the Bible passage. Print and stick the photos together to use as a reminder of the story in the following weeks. (Remember to get the permission of parents/guardians if the children are to feature in the re-enactment.)

342. Build on Your Knowledge

For older groups study a familiar passage and talk about how their understanding of this passage has changed from when they were toddlers to now. Add the next layer of their understanding for them.

Word

343. No Laughter

Tell the whole story but tell everyone in the group that no one is allowed to laugh. Work your hardest to see if you can make someone laugh.

344. Tell It with Hats

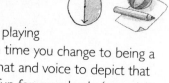

Tell the full story of the passage, playing several different characters. Each time you change to being a different character, change your hat and voice to depict that character. This should be lots of fun for everybody (especially when you get completely confused as to who you are supposed to be and use the wrong voice with the wrong hat!).

345. Points for the Goody

Compare two characters in a Bible passage. As you tell the story the group has to shout out who should get a point in each verse for doing the right thing. If one person is less righteous try and gain them as many points as possible. Relate this back to the children's own lives, illustrating the key things that God is looking for from us and challenging them to think about how they measure up to His expectations. (Don't forget to mention God's grace, too – after all, "All have sinned and fallen short of God's glory".)

346. I Am . . .

To introduce a well-known passage, tell one person who it is about. They then have to sit in the middle of the group and answer questions from the rest of the group. They are only allowed to answer 21 questions and the only answers they are allowed to give are "Yes" or "No".

347. Don't Be Distracted

Talk about the importance of your message for the day and how it is vital that the children do not get distracted. Then during the course of the group, with help from a couple of accomplices, do your utmost to distract them. Test them at the end to see how much they have grasped, and fill in any gaps.

Word

348. Who Are You Like?

Looking at the different characters in the Bible study, get the group to think about who they are most like, and why.

349. What Flavour Is It?

If this story was an item of food what food would it be and why? For example: It might be a bowl of rice, because it tells us how we should live our lives every day. It might be a chilli pepper, because it is a hot story that some people will find hard to take if they are not used to it.

350. What Colour Is It?

Choose a colour that represents the Bible passage and explain why. For example it may be black because it is a very dark story or red because it stands out from others.

Word

Visual

Word

351. Object Lesson

Choose an object that can help illustrate today's teaching point. It may be an object from around your house. For example a light needs to be plugged in to work – in the same way we need to be plugged in to God.

352. It's An Illusion

Use an illusion from your local magic shop to help illustrate the message in the passage for today. Explain to the group that it is not magic, but just an illusion, to help them understand what the Bible is saying.

353. Felt Pictures

Using felt shapes on a flannel board, tell the story.

354. Draw It

Draw the story as you tell it.

355. From A Picture Book

Using a Bible picture book, tell the story and talk about the pictures.

356. I Can't Wait

Ask the group if they have ever been in a situation where they can't wait for something to happen (e.g. for their birthday to come). Get them to describe what it was like. Go on to explain to them how different things will be when Jesus comes back. We should be expecting this to happen. To help with this sense of anticipation take a balloon and start to blow it up. With each puff of air say that Jesus is coming back soon. The children will begin to think the balloon is going to burst if you keep going – explain that as time passes Jesus will soon come back and it will be an exciting day. Set the Bible passage in the context of the fact that Jesus is coming back soon.

357. DVD Time

Show a film of the story. Get them to spot any ways in which it is different from what is actually written in the Bible. Get them to think about what things are the same. Use this opportunity to emphasize the importance of reading the Bible for yourself, to discover what it says and not just depend on what someone else thinks it says.

358. Mystery Box

This idea works well if it is used over a number of weeks. Bring a box to the group with a mystery object in it each week that will link in with the teaching. Before you take the object out of the box describe it to the group, and see if anyone can guess what it is.

359. Holy Land Photos

Bring some photos of Israel to the group to show what the places in the passage you are studying look like today. If you don't have any of your own there are plenty available on the internet.

360. Film Clip

Choose a clip from an age-appropriate film that illustrates the point you want to make. Make sure you back up your teaching point with Scripture.

361. Resources to Explain

Bring some resources with you that help explain things from Bible times. It may be a shepherd's crook to represent the Good Shepherd, or sandals to help explain how feet got dirty and Jesus washed them.

Word

Just Do It

362. Track Your Progress

Create a chart to track how each person does on remembering the take-home keys from previous weeks and doing the action point you set each week. Have prizes for the winners.

363. Enough Evidence

If you were taken to court for following Jesus would there be enough evidence to convict you? If this passage was acting as evidence then would it be evidence for or against you? Act out a court scene and get different members of the group to play different parts in the court (judge, solicitors, etc.) to get them to see how much evidence there is that they are following Jesus at school.

Word

364. Why Is It Here?

Ask why God put this passage in the Bible. What does He want us to *learn*? What does He want us to *do*?

365. What Stops You

Discuss the things that will stop you doing what God wants you to do. Look at these reasons in the light of all that God has done for us – are they reasons or are they actually excuses?

366. With God's Help

Remind the children that God is always there to help us to do what He needs us to do.

367. Prayer Focus

Turn the week's teaching into a prayer focus that you spend time praying for together, to see real growth in individual lives.

368. Your Story

Encourage the group to share their stories of situations they have faced where this passage would have been a real help to them. Knowing what they now know from the teaching, ask what they would do differently next time.

369. Where You Are

Talk about how the week's teaching can be applied in different places – at school, at home, in church and at a friend's house.

370. Reality

Talk about how it can be hard to follow God and to do the right things. What things encourage us to keep going? Is there any encouragement in this week's passage?

Word

Drama

371. Emotions

Get the group to act out the different emotions that the characters would have felt in the story.

372. Director's Cut

Get the group to act out a full version of the Bible passage, leaving nothing out. They will need to think about what the characters were doing before and after the story. Were there any bits that could have happened during the story that were not mentioned? At the end make sure it is clear what parts were in the Bible and what parts were added for dramatic effect.

373. Cut, Cut

Get the group to act out the Bible passage, then come in as the director and give directions such as "We need more emotion", "We need everybody to be happy (even those who should be sad)", or "We need everyone to be serious". Have fun changing the mood of the drama before going on to analyse what actually happened.

374. The Sequel

Get the group to think of what happened next. For example, if you are reading of how Jesus healed a person, what happened to them after they were healed? Use this to emphasize that God was touching real lives and bringing lasting change.

375. The Non-action Drama

Give each person a part from the Bible passage. They then have to act the part BUT they must speak in a monotonic voice and they are not allowed to move. This activity helps crystallize the key facts of a passage.

376. Mime It

Get the group to mime the story without making any sounds.

377. Sound Effects

As you read the Bible passage, get the group to make up sound effects that match the passage.

378. Read And Act

One person reads out the Bible passage while the other members of the group act it out, making it up as they go along.

379. Read Then Act

The whole group reads through the passage together then, in small groups, they prepare to act it out.

Word

380. Freeze Frames

These are like photographs of the story. Each member of the group takes a pose to show the story in a series of stills.

381. In Small Groups

Divide everyone into small groups and give each group a different section of the story to act out. Give them time to work out their section of the story then get the groups to act out their section from beginning to end.

Have hats for the key characters to wear so that the story is easier to follow for those watching as the different sections are acted out.

382. Modern Dilemma

From the Bible passage, work out the key message and turn it into a modern dilemma for the group to act out. For example, if you are teaching from Matthew 5:39 on turning the other cheek, set an example where someone comes and knocks your books out of your hand. What might happen next? When the different versions of the scenario have been acted out turn to the Bible passage for the week and see what it has to say about your scenarios.

Art and Craft

383. Crafty Prop

Before you come to the Bible story get the children to create a prop that they can use in the story. For example they could make a palm leaf to use in the story of Palm Sunday.

384. Finger Puppets

Make finger puppets for the group to use as you share the story.

385. Craft Straws

Use craft straws to make people that each member of the group can use to act out the story as you read it to them.

386. Draw A Picture of the Story

Get each member of the group to draw a picture of the story to show to the others.

387. Colouring

Give the children a picture of the story for them to colour in. As they colour it in use the time to reinforce the message that you have taught, by talking with them about the story again.

Word

388. Craft Activity

Select a craft activity for the group
to do that will reinforce the message of the Bible story. As they are
making it, use the time to reinforce the message by talking to them
about what they are making and how this links with the story.

389. Finger Painting

Use finger painting to recreate the story for the week.
Make sure you have plenty of things to clean up
with afterwards.

390. Create A Collage of the Story

Work together to create a collage of the whole story,
using as many different materials as you can lay your
hands on. Refer back to the collage in the weeks that
follow, as you recap on the teaching.

Word

Other

391. Holy Spirit, Help Me

Read the Bible passage together as a group. Then ask everybody to make a note of what they can learn from it. Pray together and ask God to teach you something new. Then read the passage again, and see what they learn this time.

392. Multiple Headlines

Get the group to think of three headlines that sum up the things that we can learn from this week's passage.

393. Rap It

Take a key part of the passage and turn it into a rap.

394. The Question Bag

Fill a bag with pieces of paper with a different question written on each. These may be questions specific to the passage or questions that can be used for any passage. Each person takes it in turn to pull a question out of the bag and answer it. Possible questions include:

- How did today's teaching impact you?

- What will you do differently as a result of today's teaching?

- What surprised you about what we have been talking about today?

- How does today's teaching make you feel?

- Can you recite the memory verse for today?

395. Choose A Song

Choose a song that links to the theme for the week. It may be a song linked directly with the story, or it may be a song that emphasizes the key teaching point. Teach the song, perhaps even with actions, and use it as a hook to help the children remember what to do.

396. Characters from History

Bring an example from history of a man, or woman, of God who applied today's teaching and explore the effects that it had on their life and ministry.

397. What Is the Truth?

Tell your group that your name is really something different from what it actually is. See how they respond. They will probably be confused. Keep this going for much of the time together, correcting them if they call you by your actual name. When you get to the Word section, tell them how you were being silly and they were right about your name all along. Some may have started to believe you by this stage. Talk about how confusing it was for them and ask them why they did not take more of a stand about what they knew was true. Develop these themes further to apply them to the ultimate truth of the Bible and the need to make a stand for our Christian faith.

Word

398. DIY Quiz

Divide the group into two teams. Give each team a pile of blank cards and challenge them to write as many questions (and corresponding answers) as they can, in five minutes. If you like, they can be based on a previous week's teachings.

Select a 'valid' question from one team and direct the question to the other team. The process continues until all 'valid' questions written by both teams have been asked.

The teams score one point for every question they answer correctly and another point for every one of their questions which you count as 'valid'.

399. Round-the-room Quiz

Create a multiple-choice quiz where the answers can be A, B or C. Put these three letters up around the room, on three different walls. As you read out the question and the possible answers each person has to go and stand next to the letter that they think represents the right answer.

400. Sermon Illustrations

Search the internet for sermon illustrations that tie in with the week's theme and are suitable to share with the children.

401. Word Search

Make a word search, with all the key words from the Bible passage, to reinforce the message for the day.

402. It's A Rabbit

Bring a toy rabbit (or indeed any object) to the group for a discussion on the passage. Only the person holding the rabbit is allowed to talk; everyone else has to wait until they have the rabbit passed to them.

403. Sticker Recap

Recap on the message for the day by asking a series of questions. Whoever gets the answers right earns a sticker. If you want to be even more sophisticated, why not give them points that can be turned into prizes every couple of months!

404. Keep Fit

Explain that the Bible helps us to keep spiritually fit, but we actually have to read it and act on it for it to take effect. Now, as you read the Bible and teach the lesson, have everybody doing keep-fit exercises, to reinforce that they have to act on what they hear.

405. Read It

Go round the group, allowing each person to read one verse. For a fun alternative pair people up and get each pair to read alternate words of a verse.

406. Don't Breathe

After you have explained the message for the week, ask one person to explain it again. While they are explaining it, everyone else has to hold their breath. Can they explain everything before anyone collapses on the floor?

407. Speak and Respond

Make up a phrase containing the key teaching point (or use a key Bible verse from the passage). During the course of the session call out the first part of the phrase —at this moment everyone has to stop what they are doing, stand up, and say the second half.

408. Balloon

Blow up a balloon as you tell the story.
When you get to the end of the story tie off the balloon and pat it over to one of the group. That person then has to answer a question on the meaning of the passage, whilst keeping the balloon in the air. When they have answered the question correctly they pat the balloon on to someone else, for them to answer the next question.

409. Unscramble Me

Scramble up the letters in some of the key words for today's teaching. Then race to see who can unscramble all of them first. This can be done both as an introduction to the teaching for the week and as a reinforcement of the teaching you have just given.

410. Hangman

Play 'Hangman' to see if the group can work out a key memory verse for the day.

411. Bible Quiz

Split the group into two teams, and have them play against each other in a Bible quiz. Choose the questions based on the age, and level, of your group. Have a prize ready for the winning team. You can make this fun by having an imaginary buzzer that they have to press if they know the answer.

Word

Younger Children

412. A Sheet

Bring an ordinary bed
sheet to the session and use it throughout the story. For example: If
the children stand under it you can wave it around to create a windy
scene on a boat; children can hide under it to turn it into a cave,
house or confined space; they can sit on it to have a picnic.

413. Puppets

Use puppets to act
out the story.

414. Puppet Narrator

Use a puppet as a narrator to help tell the story.

415. Move Around

As you tell the story move to
different areas of the room for different parts of the story.
One part may represent someone's house, another may
be the tree the characters pass in the story.

416. Action Time

As you tell the story, choose
up to five key words or characters. Whenever you say these
words the children have to do an associated action.

417. Key Objects

Bring key objects that are mentioned in the story to the group for them to hold up and pass round as you tell the story. The children can describe each object as they hold it.

418. Silly Billy

As you tell the story change some of the words so that the children have to correct you. For example, "Jonah was swallowed by a big *mouse*", or "To show Noah that He'd never flood the earth again, God put a *helicopter* in the sky".

419. Happy Face, Sad Face

Draw a sad face and a happy face on two different sheets of paper. The children have to call out if the story, a character in the story, or God, is happy, or sad, at different parts of the story. Hold up the appropriate face.

420. I'll Say It

Choose five children, and give them key words that are part of the story. They may be words that are very important in the story, or they may be the name of a key character in the story. Give them a card to hold. Whenever you need one of the words during the telling of the story, tap the head of the person holding the card. They can then hold the card up and everyone can say the word on it.

421. Costumes

Bring costumes for the children to dress up in to act out the story.

Word

Warfare

Contents

Introduction

During this section the aim is that those under your care will engage in the spiritual realm, through prayer. God has given us incredible access to His throne room, to be able to ask anything in Jesus' name. Such authority should not be taken lightly – it is a privilege God has given us, but the role of the intercessor is also one of responsibility.

So the aim is not that anyone in the group will 'say prayers', but rather that they will actually pray, entering the throne room of God. As with the worship time, it is an attitude of heart that is required and again you will need to lead by example. So, if you want them to be strong in prayer, you will need to spend time in prayer for them during the week.

The overall aim is that each of the young disciples in our care will be intercessors, not just on a Sunday, but every day. Developing a regular habit of prayer, as well as turning to prayer as an instinct in every circumstance and situation, will allow God to step in and be a part of their everyday lives.

Of course prayer is not just about talking to God, it is also about listening to God's heart. We don't just pray to feel good – we pray because we want God to answer. Encourage each person to share the ways that God answers their prayer. Encourage them not only to see specific answers to prayer, but also to see how they have changed by establishing a regular habit of prayer.

Expect to see God move in great ways as you build this area of their spiritual lives.

Warfare

Prayer Games

422. Find the Prayer Points

Hide prayer points around the room and tell everyone to find them. As they find each one, they can take a moment to pray for what is suggested. They should then put it back, for others to find, before going on to look for the next prayer point.

423. Power to Pray

Get the group to choose three friends who do not follow Jesus and to pray for them. As they do this, give them a balloon. Each time they pray they should blow one puff into the balloon, until the balloon bursts. There are some things we have to keep on praying for, like the salvation of our friends, until God answers us.

Alternatively, for those who can't cope with bursting balloons, they can add weights to an elastic band until it snaps, or books to a piece of card until it crumples under the weight.

424. Give Thanks

Because of the cross, our lives have been changed. Using the letters 'THE CROSS', thank God for as many things as you can think of. The group leader calls out the letter 'T' and the group starts to thank God for things beginning with 'T'. Help them to pray not, for example, for their Telephone, as we want to develop deeper prayer lives than only seeing the materialistic world around them, but instead they can pray for things like: 'Taking care of me', 'Transforming my nature', 'Telling me about Jesus', and so on. Move along to the next letter, 'H', and repeat the exercise before going on to use the remaining letters one by one.

425. Together We Stand

Each group member will pray two sentences. When the first person finishes, he or she calls the name of another group member and they continue the prayer.

This goes on until everyone has prayed or the time has run out.

426. Whisper A Prayer

Focus on one item for your prayer agenda today. Whisper it in the ear of one person. That person prays quietly about it. After a short prayer, they then pass on the prayer topic, whispering it into the ear of somebody else. They then pray quietly, so no one else will hear what they are praying for, then they pass it on to someone else. When everyone has had an opportunity to whisper a prayer, the last person tells the group what he or she prayed for. Is it the same as what was first whispered?

427. Thank God for . . .

Get the group to sit in a circle. The first person thinks of something to thank God for (e.g. their parents) and says "Thank you, God, for my parents." The next person does the same but includes the first person's thanksgiving request as well: "Thank you, God, for my parents and this group." The third person adds their own item to be thankful for on to the list, repeating all the other things that have been said. Keep going round the group, adding more things until people cannot remember the list anymore.

428. Prayer Ball

Using a ball, get the group each to pray one at a time. When they are holding the ball they have to pray. Everyone else can agree by saying "Amen". Then they throw the ball to someone else who has a turn to pray.

429. Aeroplane Prayers

Give the group some paper to make paper aeroplanes with. On them they can write some prayers or the names of the people from their Prayer of Three (see Active Prayers, no. 473). When they have made the aeroplanes they can throw them as they pray the prayer on them. They can then run to pick up someone else's plane and pray the prayer on that plane as they throw it across the room.

430. Hopping Prayer

Explain that the Bible says we should pray with thanksgiving. Get the group to stand on one leg and to thank God for everything. Then they can jump on to the other leg and ask God for things. Every time you shout out "Change!" they should change between their thanking leg and their asking leg.

Warfare

Visual Prayers

431. God's Vision

Pray together, asking God to show His vision for each person's life. Get the children to draw or write down what God shows them.

432. Tipping the Scales

Make a chart which shows a scale of 0–10. Get the group to think about one part of the fruit of the Spirit. If 10 means showing this part of the fruit all the time, even when under pressure, and 0 means never showing it, how highly would they score? They can mark their score on the chart. Are there times when they score less? If there are get them to pray about those times and ask the Lord to give them more of that part of the fruit.

Go through the other parts of the fruit of the Spirit. Let the group know how you score too – this will show them that you are not perfect (and will help prevent them from thinking that they score 10/10 on all aspects of the fruit!).

433. Prayer Stations

Set up four stations around the room, each containing something different to pray for. Have photographs, Scripture or prayer ideas at each one. Split the group into four, each group standing at one of the stations. Let them pray for two minutes at the station, then move them round to the next one until they have visited all four stations.

434. Prayer with Thanksgiving

Bring two pieces of card, each of a different colour, to the group. Tell them that when you hold up one card they should ask God for things, then when you hold up the other card they should thank God. Alternate between the two cards.

435. Parts of the Body

Pray for different topics, using your body as a guide for each topic. For example: Head – studies at school; Feet – safety where we go; Legs – family who support us; Heart/chest – relationship with God. Each person can touch the part of the body you call out as they pray for that topic.

436. Give

On a large sheet of paper, let the group write or draw something that they are willing to give to God. Also bring some pictures of other things that people have given to God. Take time to give Him these things where possible. Lead this into a time of intercession.

437. Sweet and Bitter

Bring some sweet food and some bitter food to the session. Let the children taste the different foods, not forgetting to check in advance for allergies. Explain that some things in life are nice; other things are not so nice. God wants us to pray about all things. Encourage them to think about their lives and others. They can then pray some sweet prayers – prayers of blessing; and some bitter prayers – prayers of deliverance.

438. Visual Prayers

Pray for the lost. Then the children can use paper and paint/crayons to draw what they see going on in the Spirit. Discuss the pictures, then use them to pray some more. If they see things changing as they pray, they can change their pictures.

439. Remove the Mask

Give each child a mask to decorate, to show how they think other people see them. Talk about whether how people see them is different from who they really are. Pray together that the mask will be removed.

440. One Brick at A Time

Talk about how the Church is made up of people, not bricks. That's why it's so important that each person becomes who God is calling them to be. Pray for each member of the group, one at a time, by name.

441. Home Map

Get the group to draw a map of their home. Let each room of their home represent a prayer topic. They can pray for each area and write on the map some details of what they are praying for.

Warfare

442. School Map

Bring a template of a school map to the group. Let the group take it home to fill in the blanks (with photos of key teachers, key activities, etc. – websites and prospectuses will help with this). Then encourage them to pray for the different areas of their school.

443. Blindfolded

Bring blindfolds made of paper to the group. Ask what stops people from following Jesus. Write the responses on the blindfolds. Then place each one on a person and have all the group pray for people who are blinded in that way, using those wearing the blindfolds as a point of contact, so that they will be able to see Jesus.

444. The Baton of Prayer

Create a prayer baton (like a relay baton). Stand in a circle as a group, then start by praying strong prayers over the prayer topic for the week. As you end your prayer, pass the baton to another member of the group who takes on the praying – with everyone else agreeing with the prayer. Continue until all have had an opportunity to lead the prayers.

445. Pray Today

Bring a newspaper to the group. Pray over the different news items and then cut out words from the paper to make up prayers.

446. Postbox Prayers

Make a postbox and bring it to the group. Get the group to write prayers on pieces of paper (younger children can draw their prayers), and then to pray them and post them in the box.

447. Picture It

Bring a picture of a stadium, or of your church hall. Get the group to pray, over the picture, that the Church of Jesus will fill these buildings.

448. Prayer Hat

Bring a hat to the group.
Tell the group that whoever is wearing the hat is the one who can pray; everyone else can agree with their prayer. Pass the hat around from one person to another.

449. Increase My Faith

Bring some watercress seeds to the group, with some cups. Tell them that their faith may start small like the seed, but it will grow. Plant the seeds on cotton wool in a cup (with water) and get the group to pray, each week, that their faith will increase. Watch the seeds grow over the weeks.

450. Pray over the Map

Bring a map of Israel to the group. Get the group to pray for the different countries neighbouring Israel and also for Israel itself – that there will be peace in the nation of Israel.

451. Prayer Shawls

The Jews use a prayer shawl as they pray as a reminder to keep the commandments and as a reminder of the access they have to God. Get the group to design prayer shawls that speak of their access to God. They can then wear them as they pray.

452. Bring Down the Walls

Make a wall out of paper or boxes. Write an issue that needs prayer on each box. As the group pray for each issue they can bring down the wall piece by piece.

453. Lift up Your Leaders

Bring some photos of your church leaders and the national leaders to the group. Pray together for each leader. If you can, why not invite some of your leaders to come along and be prayed for in person? Write down anything that God tells the children, and pass it on to the leaders, as appropriate.

Warfare

454. Prayer Tree

Make a tree and cut out some
paper to represent fruit. Get the group to write some
prayer requests on the pieces of paper, then hang
them on the tree.

455. Destroy the False Teachings

Ask the group what lies they have heard about God or
what false teachings their friends at school know. Compare
the teachings with what the Bible says, then write them
down on a bit of paper. Get your group to pray against
these teachings, tearing up the paper as they do so. Make
sure they actually pray and don't simply get carried away
tearing up the paper!

456. Hearer to Doer

Put up two signs in the room, one
saying 'Hearer' and the other saying 'Doer'. Explain how
we can say we want to serve God but not actually do
it. Encourage the group to think about times that they
have promised God they would do something, but then
not done it. Get them to walk from the 'Hearer' sign to
the 'Doer' sign, repenting for their inaction and asking
God to help them.

457. The Listening Wall

Put a large sheet of paper up on the wall (backing
paper used for decorating is a good, cheap way of
getting a large amount of paper). Get the group to
pray for a particular topic, like their friends who don't
know Jesus. As they pray they should listen to God,
and as He speaks they should draw, or write, what He
shows them. At the end go through everything on the
wall and discuss it with the group.

458. Blocks to Salvation

Get the children to ask God what
blocks their friends from being saved.
These may be blocks in their friends
or blocks in their own lives that stop
them from telling their friends about
God. They should then write these
down (or draw them).

Next they can pray these blocks away,
crossing them out once they feel that
God has answered their prayer.

Warfare

459. Prayer Rope

Take a piece of string, and get the group to tie knots into it. They can then work their way along the string, praying for a different person as they come to each knot.

460. The Poor Wall

Build a wall out of blocks and stick on to it pieces of paper with different prayer points for the poor written on them. Get the group to pray through these barriers for the poor. Then ask God what you, as a group, can do for the poor. (Make sure you do it, too!)

461. Repent

Think about the story of Jonah as he ran away from God. The boat was a symbol of Jonah's sin – he was running away from God in it. The fish was a symbol of God's grace – the fish rescued Jonah, even though he did not deserve to be rescued. Get the group to make a picture of themselves and a large picture of a boat and one of a fish. As they think about their sins, lead them in a time of repentance. While they repent they can walk from their sin (the boat) to God's grace (the fish).

462. Prayer for Three

Draw a picture of a river that people have to cross to get to Jesus. Let each person think of three of their friends who do not know Jesus and put their names on one side of the river. Pray for them to accept Jesus and move on to the other side. During the next few months, as each person gets saved, move the names across the river. Take a week to explain the concept to the group and keep coming back to it each week after that, to see how they are doing.

463. Culture Feature

Bring items from a country, such as food, clothes and photos, or even a native. Talk about the needs of that country, and then pray together for it.

464. Pray for the Family

Encourage the group to bring in photos of different members of their family. When they have them, get the group to lay hands on the photos and pray for each person. Alternatively they can draw pictures of their family, and do the same thing.

Warfare

465. Colour Prayers

Hold up differently coloured pieces of paper, ask the group what it reminds them of and thank God for these things.

466. Use Your Hand

Use your thumb and each finger of your hand to bring to mind different things to pray for.

- **Thumb:** This is the **strongest** digit on your hand. Give thanks for all the strong things in your life, like home and family; relationships that support and sustain you.

- **Index finger:** This is the **pointing** finger. Pray for all those people and things in your life who guide and help you. Friends, teachers, doctors, nurses, emergency services and so on.

- **Middle finger:** This is the **tallest** finger. Pray for all the important people who have power in the world, like members of parliament and local councillors, the Royal Family, other world leaders and their governments.

- **Ring finger:** This is the **weakest** finger on your hand. It cannot do much by itself. Remember the poor, the weak, the helpless, the hungry, the sick, the ill and the bereaved.

- **Little finger:** This is the **smallest**, and the **last**, finger on your hand. Pray for yourself.

467. Grateful

Get some pictures of people who are having a difficult life. You can find pictures from newspapers, or the internet, of hungry children, homeless people, people living in an area of natural disaster, etc. Discuss how hard life is for those in the pictures. Now ask who would appreciate food and shelter more. Will it be you, who have always had these things, or the hungry and homeless? No doubt it will be the hungry and homeless.

Explain to the group that because most of them were brought up in churches, they may not have experienced a wide variety of sinful acts. Therefore, when compared with someone who has had a lot of bad experiences and then become a Christian, the person with the many bad experiences is more likely to be more grateful to God for the changes He has made in their life.

Why not imagine for a moment what your life could have been like if you did not know Jesus? Now that you have a picture, worship God for His wonderful change. Give Him praise for delivering you both from sin and from the results of sin.

Warfare

468. Letter

Write a letter to God asking for His help to keep following Him. Write down the things you are finding hard about following God as you ask Him for help.

469. Build A Prayer Wall

Get the group to write down prayer requests and thanksgivings on pieces of paper of different colours (to be used as coloured bricks). Allocate one colour for requests and a different one for thanksgivings. Let each person stick these 'bricks' onto a large piece of paper, to make a prayer wall, praying the prayers as they do so. Look at the colour of the wall – is it made up of mainly thanksgiving, or mainly asking God for things, or is there a balance between the two?

470. Ribbon Prayers

Bring ribbons of different colours to the group. Give each group member a ribbon of a different colour. They can tie this to their wrist as they pray for a topic. The ribbon will remind them to keep on praying. You may want to use different colours for different types of prayer. E.g. red for salvation of friends, white for holiness, green for thanksgiving.

471. One at A Time

Ask each member of the group for one thing they would like to pray for and write these on a board or large sheet of paper. Work your way through the list together praying for one thing at a time.

472. Prayer Cards

Bring some prayer cards to the group and encourage the children to fill the cards in with their requests. The cards could also be used evangelistically: they can ask their friends what to pray for and fill in a prayer card on their behalf, bringing it back to be prayed for by the group. When God answers they may well have an opening to share the Gospel with their friend.

Warfare

Active Prayers

473. Prayer of Three

Use the 'Prayer of Three' rap in your group as a way of letting each person pray for three of their friends who do not yet know Jesus:

1, 2, 3, I'm praying for my 3.
1, 2, 3, I'm praying for my 3.
1, 2, 3, I'm praying for my 3.
They're going to get saved, saved, saved;
they're going to get saved, saved, saved;
they're going to get saved, saved, saved,
as I pray.

Name ...I'm praying for you.
Name ...I'm praying for you.
Name ...I'm praying for you.
You're going to get saved, saved, saved;
you're going to get saved, saved, saved;
you're going to get saved, saved, saved,
as I pray.

(Bridge)
Satan you're defeated;
Satan you're defeated;
Satan you're defeated,
as I pray.

474. Circle Prayers

Get the group to stand in a circle, and turn so they are facing someone else's back. They can then pray for the person in front of them. Then, when you say so, they can turn 180 degrees to pray for the person on the other side of them.

475. Prayer March

March around the room together praying for three friends who they want to know Jesus. As they march they are like an army, going out to battle to fight for their friends' souls.

Warfare

476. Praying Positions

In the Bible we read that people prayed standing up, lying down, kneeling or sitting, with their hands in the air or by their side. Discuss what some of these different positions show. Get the group to pray different prayers in the different positions.

477. Level of Passion

Pray through different topics. As the children pray encourage them to change their position, depending on how passionately they feel about the topic. For example, they could sit, stand, raise their arms or kneel.

478. Prayer Walk

Take your group on a prayer walk around the local area. Don't forget to make sure you have the right ratio of adults to children as you go and that parents know what you are up to!

479. In-Out

Ask everyone to stand in a circle, facing towards the middle. Tell them to pray for those in the group. Some people may want to share specific things that they would like prayer for.

When you have done this ask the group to turn and face outwards, to pray for those who are not yet part of the Church. You may want to lay hands on the walls of the room and pray that people will come and join the group.

Warfare

Promoting Prayer

480. Daily Prayer

Encourage each person to pray daily for as many minutes a day as they are years old. So five-year-olds pray for five minutes a day and eleven-year-olds for eleven minutes a day. Set them the challenge to do this on their own at home seven days a week. Follow up on this challenge the next week, to find out how many days out of seven they prayed for their full allocation of minutes. Encourage them to persist in this and continue following up each week until they have established a regular pattern of individual prayer at home. For those who are struggling, why not call them midweek to find out how they are getting on and encourage them to pray after you have called them? After a few months, give some time to talk about the benefits and the challenges they have found from having more regular prayer times.

481. Bible Declaration

For each prayer point get the group to find a Bible verse that will act as fuel for prayer. If they find this hard you can encourage them on the need to know the Bible well.

482. Freedom

We have freedom to pray in this country. Share stories of those who don't, then encourage the children to make the most of their freedom and to pray strongly today.

483. Exercise Faith

Choose an area to pray for where the children can exercise faith. It may be someone who is sick, or it may be another situation. Whatever it is make sure you encourage the group to hear from God about the matter and to believe what He says. Then provide feedback to the group when the prayers are answered.

484. Real Prayer

Talk about how we can be fake in our prayers and just pray religious prayers. Or we can express to God how we are really feeling. A quick glance through the book of Psalms shows us that God wants us to be real with Him. He then helps us to work through our emotions and shows us His angle on things.

485. Prophesy

Encourage the group to pray and then prophesy over each other.

486. Listen and Obey

Tell everyone to pray and ask God to give them a task for the week. This may be something that they have to do, or something that they need to change. Stress the importance of obeying God. Write down each thing that God says to each member of the group. Remind them of it midweek, and follow up on it the week after to see how they got on.

487. Spirit-Led

Pray together as a group to ask God what He wants you to pray for. Follow His prayer agenda for the day. This is a great way to teach your group more on how to flow with the Holy Spirit.

488. Extended Prayer

Set aside an extended time of prayer, praying until you have a breakthrough in the things you are praying for.

489. Interpret It

Pray in tongues over an issue, then when you have prayed for a while switch to praying for the same thing in English. Afterwards ask the group if they prayed anything that they did not expect over the situation when they prayed in English, or if God said anything to them while they were praying in tongues.

490. LOVE

Ask the group to think of times when they have not been as loving as they should have been. Give them an opportunity to repent for these times and to ask God to give them His heart for people.

491. Ministry in the Spirit

Minister to each of your group members as the Spirit leads you, laying hands on them and praying for them.

Warfare

492. God's Word

Present a current issue to the group
and together ask God to give a word of wisdom,
or a word of knowledge, to help guide the
prayers for this matter.

493. Pray the Word

Take a passage of Scripture and
encourage the group to pray it over their lives. You may
want to get hold of a copy of *God's Word in my Mouth*,
by Colin Dye, to help with some Scriptural prayers.

494. Open-heart Surgery

Let the Holy Spirit speak to each person, telling
them areas of their lives where God is not in charge. After
this encourage the group to repent and put God back at the
centre, in every area of their lives. Let the group members
prophesy over each other.

495. Lead It

Let the group take it in turns to
lead the Warfare time. Warn them in advance so
that they have time to pray and prepare.

496. Bible Prayers

Pray using a passage of
Scripture, for example one of the psalms.

497. Prayer of Agreement

Get the group to pray in twos or threes,
listening to each other and agreeing with each other's
prayers. Perhaps they can pray about their friends who
do not know Jesus, or about an upcoming evangelistic
event in your church, where they want to see their
friends saved.

Warfare

498. Faith Progression

Choose an issue to pray through. Get the group to pray and listen to God until they know that it has been answered. They should then thank God for the answered prayer and go out from the group expecting to see the answer. Talk about the answer the following week.

499. In Perspective

John came preaching that the kingdom of heaven is near. The same is true today. It is easy to focus our prayers on our needs, but take time to focus prayers on kingdom priorities – souls being saved, groups being planted.

500. Spiritual Warfare

Take an issue and pray it through until the point of breakthrough. Use this as an opportunity to demonstrate to your group more about intercession and how they can pray through issues at home.

501. One-minute Stints

Get the group to pray in tongues for one-minute stints. Talk about how this builds us up, or edifies us. Repeat this a few times in the group then get them to listen to God.

502. Wait on God

Get the group to talk to God about an area and then to spend time listening to Him – waiting on Him. Talk about what God said to each of them, and help them to discern whether or not it was actually God.

503. THE Need

Ask the group what one thing they really want to pray for. As well as telling you where they are at with God, this will give them an opportunity to pray for real issues.

Warfare

504. Speaking in Tongues

The Bible says that when we speak in tongues we edify ourselves (1 Corinthians 14:4). Teach the children about the gift of tongues and, if they don't speak in tongues, give them an opportunity to receive the gift. Spend some time as a group doing some spiritual weightlifting: speak in tongues to edify yourself and become spiritually stronger. Remember Paul said that he spoke in tongues more than all the Corinthians (1 Corinthians 14:18), so if we have the gift we need to use it in our prayer times with God.

505. How to Have A Quiet Time

Lead the group to pray as if they were at home on their own, instead of praying as a group. As you guide them you can model to them what they can do when they are at home with God.

506. Jesus Is Coming Back Soon

Get the group to pray for a topic as you tell them to. They should all pray together, but when each child has finished saying their prayers they should start to chant "Jesus is coming back soon". As they finish their prayers more and more children will join in with this until everyone is saying it. It can then get louder and louder. Then get the group to pray for a new topic in the same way. Explain how we should think every day about the fact Jesus is coming back soon.

507. 30 Seconds

Give the group a topic to pray for but give them only 30 seconds to pray for it. As soon as the 30 seconds is up give them another topic. Continue this until the time is up.

508. Impartation

Go round your group one at a time and lay hands on each person. Pray that they will encounter God as you pray for them. Prophesy over them as God leads you.

509. Unknown Tongue

Having chosen your prayer agenda, discuss with your group the benefits of sustained continuous attack in a battle. Encourage them to apply this as they pray. They can choose to use 'speaking in unknown tongues' as their only weapon throughout the Warfare session. Support those who are not experienced in this and give opportunities for them to receive this gift.

Warfare

510. Prayer and Praise

Have carefully selected praise music available for this time. During the time of prayer, play the praise music in the background. This will help the group to enter into God's presence as they join with the anointed worship, supported by the praises being given to Him.

511. Hands On

Get the group to pray for each other, laying hands on each other and praying for blessing and protection in each other's lives.

512. Prayer Cover

Organize the children into groups of three. Get them to pray for each other in those groups and then to continue to pray for each other during the week. Every week they can pray in their groups to provide prayer cover.

513. Requests with Thanksgiving

As a group, list some things to pray to God for. Then pray for each one, but tell the group that they have to ask God for these things while thanking Him. Explain the importance of being grateful to God for these things. E.g. if you are praying for good results in exams, thank God for the opportunity to be in school to learn; if you are praying for a bully, thank God that you can know him and so have an opportunity to pray for him.

514. Listen Up

Prayer is a two-way conversation with God. We speak and God listens. God speaks and we listen, just like when we are on the telephone. Take some time to listen to God – He may have things He wants you to pray for, or do. Or He may simply want to tell your group something.

515. PUSH

Choose a prayer topic and pray it through until you get a breakthrough (e.g. praying for unsaved friends to come to Jesus). As the acronym says: PUSH (Pray Until Something Happens).

Warfare

Prayer Topics

516. STOP Prayer

Lead everyone to pray the STOP prayer:

- They should say **Sorry.**

- They should **Thank** God.

- They should pray for **Others.**

- They should ask God '**Please?**' for their own requests.

517. Repentant Prayer Time

Call each member of the group to repent for the way they have treated somebody. Then get them to write a letter to that person (maybe a parent, teacher or friend) to say sorry.

518. Different Religions

Encourage the group to pray for those of different religions, that they will come to know Christ. You may want to tell stories of people from other faiths who have come to know Christ.

519. The Beatitudes

Pray through each one of the Beatitudes, as a group, asking for each of the characteristics Jesus speaks of.

520. Remember, God, that . . .

Encourage everyone to pray, remembering prophetic words God has given them – things He has done in the past, or things He said He would do in His Word. "Remember, God, that you said ... and we believe you. Let it happen."

521. Tear Down the Lies

Tear down false ideologies – what things in life do their generation believe are against the Bible? Pray to pull down each of these things.

522. Over Me

Lead the group into God's presence, through prayer and worship. Then encourage them to pray for each other and listen to God. When they hear Him say something for the person, they should share it. Encourage them to ensure it is as encouraging as Barnabas, the encourager, would want it to be.

523. Miracle God

Talk to God, asking for specific instructions of what He wants to do in their areas of influence at school and at home. Pray into the things God says. Write down each one and tick them off as they are fulfilled.

524. Pray for the Church

Using Ephesians 4:11-12 pray for the ministers of the Church called to the fivefold ministry – there to equip us. Then pray to the rest of the saints that we will do the work of the ministry as God has called us to.

525. The Fivefold Ministry

Pray for each of the fivefold ministries, that God will raise them up and that their roles will be fulfilled in the Church. So for example: "We pray that the Evangelists will be raised up, and that the lost will hear the Gospel through all people. That the Pastors will be raised up, and that people will experience God's care through the Church."

526. Be Bold

Lead the group to pray for boldness, and God's strategy, in reaching out to their friends.

527. Easter Is Coming

Look at your church's programme for Easter – is there an event that your group can target for their friends to come to? Get the group to imagine what God can do through that event. Then get them to pray those dreams into reality, since God is able to do far more than we can ask or even imagine. Encourage the children to pray especially for three of their friends who do not know Jesus to come and meet with Him.

Warfare

528. Pray for Each Other

Get the group to write down one thing that they would like prayer for in their walk with God. They can give the pieces of paper to you and you can pass the requests out to different members of the group, as appropriate. They can then pray for each other. At the end collect up all the pieces of paper and take them home as your prayer fuel for the group.

529. Take Back the City

Work together to create a list of ways that your city or village is not living up to God's best. Next to each thing write how God would want to change it. For example, instead of fighting with each other, people should start loving each other. Pray through each item together, one thing at a time.

530. Back on Fire Again

Challenge your group to consider if they have ever felt closer to God than they do right now. If they have then lead them to cry out to God that they will be near to Him once more. This should be a prayer time of heartfelt desperation, so encourage them to reflect on how far they have come and what it was like when they were close to God before.

531. A Foreign Land

Get the group to pray for the 10/40 Window nations, where most of the unevangelized people live. Up-to-date details on different countries can be found on the internet.

532. Giving

We can think of tithe in relation to giving a proportion of our money for something other than ourselves. Why not give some of the prayer time today over to the benefit of others? As we sow prayers for others, we know that others will be praying for us.

533. The Cry of the Church

Teach the children about praying for Jesus to return – then pray that the bride will be prepared and that He will return soon.

Warfare

534. For Those in Authority

Once again we need to pray for our leaders. Think of as many leaders as possible and pray that God will give them wisdom, courage and a heart that loves to offer the best for the people they lead. Include your group leader, the pastors of the church, the leaders of your country, etc.

535. Pray Through Worship

Use a revival song to pray and cry out for revival in the schools of the nation.

536. Pray for the Persecuted

Share the needs of the persecuted Church.
Some ideas for this can be found from Christian Solidarity Worldwide: http://www.csw.org.uk/

537. Pray for A Nation

Look at a nation of the world and bring in some relevant objects for the group to look at. Then tell them a bit about the needs of the nation, and pray for that nation. Operation World is a good source of prayer fuel for this. http://operationworld.24-7prayer.com/

538. Simply Pray

Pray for peace in Jerusalem, especially for her neighbours, Church leaders, political leaders and so on. Pray that Jews will discover Jesus as their saviour.

539. Rule As God Wants

The Lord's Prayer says 'Your kingdom come, your will be done, on earth as it is in heaven'. Get the children to pray for this to be true in different areas of our world and in different sectors of society, such as politics, crime, schools, areas of war or famine, etc.

540. Spiritually Poor

Ask the group who the poor are.
Get them to think too of those who don't know Jesus. These people are far worse off, as they are headed for a Christless eternity. Pray for revival in your city.

Warfare

541. Model Prayer

Use the Lord's Prayer as a model of how to pray. Go through each line of the Lord's Prayer and as you do so encourage the group to pray similar prayers:

- Access
- Adoration
- Submission
- Intercession
- Provision
- Confession
- Forgiveness
- Protection
- Deliverance

542. Bless the Bullies

Get the group to pray prayers of blessing on the school bullies. Initially they will probably not want to do this, but encourage them that we are to love our enemies and to pray for those who persecute us. This is one way they can do this.

543. Prophetic Prayer

As a group ask God what He is saying and then get them to pray for these things.

544. The Spirit of This Age

List the aspects of the season that are contrary to God's will. For example materialism, greed and gluttony are rife in the West. Get the group to pray the opposite things into the world.

545. No Worries

Ask the group members what things are worrying them. Get the whole group to pray for each of these things and to pray that they won't be worried, but will trust God instead.

546. Give Thanks

In pairs, share with each other how God has been good to you in the past year. Try to avoid asking God for anything today.

Warfare

547. Evangelism of Three

The Evangelism of Three is a tool to encourage each member of the group to target their prayers at three of their non-Christian friends, for them to be saved, and to share Jesus with them.

The details: Each group member makes a list of ten non-Christians they know and chooses three of them to pray specifically for, as God leads them. The group members can get together in threes to pray for their threes.

The key: The key is to keep the Evangelism of Three as a focus of the group each week. Follow up commitments that they make to speak to their friends and encourage positive results. Give time in group to praying for the lost and each week mention the Prayer of Three in some form. Be an encourager and be an example to your group. If you remember it your group will, if you don't they won't.

Use some tools: Have ways of visually representing the three to your group. Use bookmarks and cards for them to record their three. Be creative in helping them grasp the importance of seeing their friends saved and celebrate each victory as a group along the way, however small it may be.

Use your times together to encourage outreach to the Evangelism of Three through roleplay, or why not organize an evangelistic event as a group to which their three friends can be invited?

Warfare

548. Bring Them In

Thank God for the work He is doing in the hearts of those you are praying for to get saved.

549. Drainpipe

Get the group to pray for each other.
They can use the drainpipe way of praying – one hand up to God, and one hand towards the person they are praying for. They can then picture the Holy Spirit flowing through them as though through a drainpipe; after all, God can use them. Don't forget, as they pray for each other, they can also prophecy into each other's lives.

Christmas

550. The Lost

Jesus' whole focus in coming to earth was to save the lost. Take time this Christmas to pray for the lost to come to know Him. Pray specific prayers for friends, and general prayers for nations.

551. Christmas Joy

Discuss with the group those for whom Christmas is not a happy time. Pray for these people.

552. Prayer Stars

Get the group to make stars from paper and to decorate them with tinsel. Prepare a template for younger children. When they have done this you can write Christmas prayers to Jesus on the stars.

553. Gluttony

Show the group a selection of toys and a picture of the cross. Explain how many people miss what Christmas is all about. They may get nice presents, but if they do not know that Jesus died for them on the cross they are worse off than someone who gets no presents at all but who knows Jesus. The presents are meant to remind us how much we can celebrate that Jesus came to the earth to save us from our sin. Pray this through as a group.

554. Christmas Picture Prayer

Using a Christmas tree, let each part represent a different prayer point. For example, the tree itself could be the need for salvation; the lights could be prayer for the evangelists; presents under the tree could be those who do not have any food/water this Christmas, etc.

555. Christmas Blues

Pray for those around the world who will not be enjoying a happy Christmas. It may be that they don't know Christ or perhaps because they are living in poverty.

Warfare

Prayer Records

556. My Prayer List

Discuss as a group what things we should try and pray for every day. Build up a prayer list together and pray for each of the things on the list.

557. Prayer Wall

Put up a prayer wall on which anyone in the group can write specific prayer requests. As the months go on, refer back to the prayer wall to see how the prayers are being answered. As prayers are answered stick the word 'ANSWERED' over the top of the prayer request. Thank God, as a group, for the answers to their prayers.

558. Group Prayer Record

Get a prayer diary, in which to record everything you pray for as a group. Over time you can look back and see how God has answered the prayers you prayed together.

559. 'Prayer Works' Diary

Create a 'Prayer Works' diary for your group. Each week write in it the things that you pray for each other. Then the following week review the prayers to see how many God has already answered. If you continue this over several months the group will see how God works.

560. Prayer Chart

Give a copy of the prayer chart to each member of your group. Let them record how they pray each day.

My Prayer Chart

My Name: _____

Warfare

	How long I prayed for	What I prayed for	What I read in the Bible	What God said to me
Monday				
Tuesday				
Wednesday				
Thursday				
Friday				
Saturday				
Sunday				

Witness

Contents

Introduction

We are called to be outward looking. By focussing on this each week, you are giving the members of the group an opportunity to exercise their faith, and a focus for their prayers.

If many in your group are not yet passionate for God, then you may want to use this time to give them an opportunity to follow God for themselves. We don't want the children and young people to feel they *have* to share the Gospel, rather they should *want* to share it because of their experience of the Lord.

Once they have opened their hearts to Him it is good to encourage them to put their faith into action, using some of the suggestions given in this section. As you encourage them to share their faith, they will also need you to be covering them in prayer.

Make sure that you also attempt anything that you challenge them to do, and report back to them, allowing them to know your successes and your failures. Sharing failures can be an encouragement to those who are trying but feel like they are not getting anywhere. However if all of the stories are those of failure then it is time to get on your knees and ask God to enrich this aspect of the group, so that as a group you will be fruitful for God's kingdom.

As you throw out the challenge to reach out consciously, be prepared to see the fruit of all that you are investing in your group in the other sections of the meeting. Rejoice together in the fruit. Remember, getting saved is not the end point; now their friends will need discipling. Prepare for a great journey ahead as you disciple those who disciple their friends, taking what you feed them and passing it on to those who are looking to them for spiritual growth.

Witness

Let's Talk

561. The Persecuted

Talk about what you can do as a group to help the world's persecuted Christians.

562. It's Raining

Think of different ways that you find out it is raining: You experience it; someone who you trust tells you about it; you see someone who has been soaked by it. Based on this, now think of different ways that our friends can find out about Jesus.

563. Be Yourself

Encourage the group to be like Jesus this week. By being who God has made them to be, they will draw others to Him.

564. Invite Them

Talk together about strategies that you can use to invite friends to church.

565. Why Are You Here?

Ask the group why God does not take us straight to heaven once we are saved: if He did we would avoid the misery of the world. But our purpose is to stay so that the lost can see God.

566. Apologetics Manual

Make a list of the hardest questions that people in the group are asked about God. Then create a manual on how to answer them with facts. A book like Josh McDowell's *Evidence That Demands a Verdict* may be of help to you for this.

Witness

567. Love Is . . .

Ask the group to define what love is. When they have come up with definitions suggest "Love is ... stopping someone from going to hell". Discuss how love should be the motive for us reaching out to our friends.

568. Links in the Chain

Ask the group what things a person does around the time that they get saved. Items on the list may include: They go to church; they pray the sinner's prayer; they hear the Gospel. Write each of these things on a separate piece of paper. Then let the group put them in the order they think each of these things happen. Go on to explain that these things can happen in any order – we just need to do our bit in telling others and encouraging them each step of the way.

569. What Next?

Talk about what happens after we have led our friends to the Lord. There is more to it than simply praying a prayer; now the baby believers need to be taught the basics of the faith and be brought into fellowship with other believers. Give them the practical tools they need to be able to do this.

570. Are You A Christian?

Ask the group whether their friends know that they are a Christian. If they do know, how do they know? Do our actions back up the words we speak?

571. Seven Reasons

Here are seven reasons why children and young people should share the Gospel with their friends:

1. Jesus loves young people. He has a special passion for the young. More than 8 out of 10 who are saved receive Christ before the age of 15.

2. Everyone is there. School is mandatory in most nations, so most will pass through in the early years of their lives.

3. The missionaries are already in place. They already know the language and there are no visa problems. They just have to find out that they ARE missionaries.

4. Young people build strong relationships in school that make evangelism much simpler than later in life.

5. There are MANY opportunities during a school year to gather students and to communicate the Good News.

6. The Word of God has time to work. If the good seed is planted, the time will come when it will grow – even if it is not until years later.

7. A move has already begun. This is a kairos moment in Europe, and no doubt in other parts of the world as well.

Witness

572. Conversation Starters

Get the group to think of as many different ways as they can to start a conversation about the Gospel.

573. Testimonies

Ask the group to share testimonies of how God has used them, so far this year, to reach out to their friends. Let this encourage the less active members that they, too, can reach out.

574. Sharing to Leading

There is often a big gap between telling our friends about God and leading them to God. At some point you need actually to ask somebody if they want to follow Jesus. Talk about how the children can do this, and ask them to share examples of how they went from sharing God with someone to actually leading them to Him.

575. From Group to School

Discuss together what happens in the group meetings that helps to prepare us to tell our friends about Jesus.

576. Put God First

Encourage each person to put God first at school, thereby choosing to be different. Through this people will see the difference between those who put God first and those who don't.

577. Witness Shapes

Use different shapes to show different aspects of the Gospel. Work out together how they can be used and then use them in evangelism. For example: A circle speaks of God's love around us the whole time; a triangle marks out the three parts of the Trinity that make up God.

578. Don't Do It

Think of ten ways to put your friends off Jesus so that they will NOT be won to Christ.

Witness

579. Dot to Dot

A dot-to-dot picture is made up of dots which need to be linked. What are the basic dots making up the Gospel that can be joined to create the full picture of what God has done? (God made the world; everybody has sinned, etc.) Our job is to share the different key dots with our friends so that they can create the picture of salvation in their own lives. If one of the dots is missing their pictures will be skewed, or incomplete.

580. Dream Time

Let each person dream of how the gifts can be used to witness to others. Then share together what God could do.

581. The Power of Persistence

Before someone gets saved they hear the Gospel, on average, around 17 times. It is important that we keep on sharing with our friends. Encourage each member of your group to share the Gospel in some way, with the same person, every school day this week. Next week follow up and see how the persistence paid off, or indeed if more persistence is still needed. Talk about different ways that they can share with their friends and let them know that it will take courage, faith and boldness. Have a time of prayer in preparation for this.

582. Don't Argue

Discuss with the group how they can avoid arguments in evangelism. Some people will disagree with us but we should not end by shouting at them "You're wrong," and not speaking to them for days. Talk about how they can handle different situations and different people. Some people may want to argue; we can witness to them by the way we live our lives. Our aim is not to win arguments, but to win souls.

584. History

Discuss how God has worked out salvation through the lives of the Israelites, with prophecies from many years ago being fulfilled. Use this to demonstrate the truth of the Gospel, and to equip the group for discussions with their non-Christian friends.

Interestingly the oldest religion is said to be Hinduism – yet the highest caste of this, the Brahmin caste, seems to stem from a holy man. Hebrew writing is without vowels. So 'Brahmin' is rendered 'Brhmn' in Hebrew – the same as the name Brhmn (alias Abraham). Research suggests that Hinduism started from around where Abraham was living, thus Abraham could be the man that Hindus look to. In the highest caste the belief is that there is only one God (who is broken up into many gods for the simpler, lower castes to understand). So if Abraham was indeed the inspiration for the Hindus, this provides further evidence that the Jews are the oldest religion, with their revelation coming from God (though being distorted by various other religions along the way).

583. In Summary

Let the group work out a phrase that summarizes everything that God has called us to do. For example: To love God and love each other.

585. Time Limit

Get different members of the group to attempt to tell the Gospel in different time frames: 2 minutes, 1 minute, 30 seconds and 10 seconds. What are the key parts of the Gospel that should be mentioned even when there is only a 10-second time frame? What are the more in-depth things you can say when you have 2 minutes to say it in?

586. The Evangelists' Ten Commandments

Work together as a group to create 'Ten Commandments for an Evangelist'. Then talk about how this will influence what they do in school. For example commandment number one may be: 'Never miss an opportunity to share the Gospel'.

587. If You Were to Die

Get the group to think about how their friends would respond if they were to ask them about life after death. As a group work out how God would want you to respond to each of these responses. Then go and share!

588. Time to Impact

Get the group to discuss how different people have impacted their lives. Usually people have done it not so much by what they have said, but by what they have done. Think about how we can impact the lives of our friends.

589. Against the Odds

Get the group to think of ways they can show the fruit of the Spirit when their friends don't. For example, if their friends are mean the group members can be kind at the same time. This example in their lives will help change their friends over time.

590. Steps of Faith

Think about the different steps that have to take place before someone becomes a Christian. For example:

1. Identify your Prayer-of-Three friends.

2. Establish contact.

3. Build the friendship.

4. Share something God has done for you.

5. Invite them to a meeting or share the Gospel with them.

6. Pray the prayer of salvation.

Get the group to think about where their friends are at, then to pray their Prayer of Three on to the next step and actively witness to them in a way that will bring them one step nearer to salvation.

Witness

591. Blocks to Receiving

Get the group to think about what stops their friends from being saved. Discuss these issues with them and then pray it through.

592. Only One Way

Use all that you know about Israel's failure to listen to God as a way to demonstrate that most religions say you have to be good enough to get to God. Only one speaks of what to do if you have already failed God. Jesus came to rescue us after we failed God. If we have never done anything wrong we can get to God any way we want. If, however, we have ever done anything wrong we need Jesus.

593. Blocks to Sharing

Get the group to think about what, if anything, stops them from sharing the Gospel with their friends. It may be fear or simply a lack of knowledge. Help them overcome these problems.

594. Sign of Salvation

Talk with the group about how the ribbon tied outside of Rahab's house, Joshua 2:18, was a sign of her salvation. We do not need an outward sign of salvation, as our sign is the Holy Spirit living in us. However we can make a sign to show people we are saved. Get the children to make up a bracelet, or a badge, that they can wear which will make people ask them what it is and give them an opportunity to share the Gospel. The badge may say, "Ask me why I'm a Christian", or "I've got good news".

595. My Testimony

Using a phone, record different members of the group as they share their testimony. These recordings can be played to friends. Don't forget to check with parents or guardians before you record their children.

596. Pointing to Jesus

Get the group to talk about how they have already pointed people to Jesus, and to think about what else they can do to carry on pointing people to Him.

Witness

597. You May But I Don't

Discuss evolution with your group. Encourage them to start conversations with their friends about evolution vs. creation. Give them the scientific facts that point to the truth of creation over and above evolution.

598. Hell

Talk about hell and why God does not want people to go there. Discuss how God has given us a role in sharing the Good News, so that people don't have to go there.

599. Do to Others

Get the group to think about Luke 6:31, "Do to others as you would have them do to you". What things would they like other people to do for them? How can the group do these things for other people?

600. Alphabet Witness

Using each letter of the alphabet, encourage the group to think of as many ways as possible to witness to their friends. Then let them choose one way that they feel comfortable with to use this week. A sample of this activity may be as follows:

A – Actions

B – Bring to church

C – Counsel friends

D – Dinner for them at my house

(etc.)

601. Let Your Light Shine

Bring a candle to the group and light it (be aware of safety as you do this). Explain how our light should shine. For the candle to shine you need fuel (wax), air and heat. We need the Word, the Spirit and prayer for our light to shine.

602. Keep Planting Seed

Bring some watercress seeds to the group. If we keep watering the seed it will grow. In the same way, if we keep praying and sharing with our friends they will start to grow spiritually. If you want to, plant some seed without watering it and see what happens in the weeks to come. It is important that we keep praying for our friends as we share with them.

Witness

603. 10 Reasons Why

Get the group to think of 10
reasons why their friends should follow Jesus.

604. Both . . . And

When we witness to our friends we
need to *show* the love of Jesus as well as *tell* them
about Him. Get the group to share ways that they
show God's love at school. Talk about other things
that they could do.

605. How God Became our Friend

Ask one person to share with the others how they
became God's friend. As time allows let more of
your group also share.

606. Reap the Benefits

Discuss with the group what benefits
there are to being God's friends. Tell them they can
share these benefits with their non-Christian friends
to encourage them to become God's friends too.

607. God Wants to Be Your Friend

Many people think God is irrelevant and has nothing
to do with them, or that He is so powerful that we
can never know Him. Rather, God wants to be our
friend and knows the details of our everyday lives.
Discuss how we can use our knowledge of God's
interest in people to share Him with our friends. For
example, if they feel sad or sick, if they blaspheme or
do something naughty, how can we bring God to
them at these times? Get the group to use role play
to show how they would respond in these different
situations.

608. The Final Encounter

One day we will all have to stand before
God. Will that encounter be a good one
or a bad one? Encourage your group to
discuss the end of time with their friends
and so lead them to Jesus.

Witness

609. World Vision

Plan as a group how you can do your bit in world missions.

610. Key Verses

Get the children to look up key verses from the Bible that they can use to share the Gospel with their friends. Set the task for them to learn these verses in the coming weeks.

611. God Is Speaking

Read 1 John 1:5-9. Discuss how you can use this to tell others about Jesus. Agree to share it with people this week.

612. Review

Review together all that you have done, so far, this year in evangelism. Has it been successful, or not? If not have a renewed effort in prayer to see things move on in the next part of the year. If there has been some success thank God for it.

613. Perplexing Questions

Ask the group to come up with questions that they have been asked about Jesus which they have not been able to answer. Some of the group may raise issues that they are struggling with themselves. Set time aside to answer these questions from the Bible.

614. Religious Focus

Spend some time in your group talking about a different religion and discuss how you can reach them for Jesus most effectively. Remember love and prayer are the keys to any evangelism, but for each religion you will find specific keys that will allow them to be more receptive to the Gospel message. Get the group to act on what they learn. You may want to choose a different religion each month.

Witness

615. Keep on Sharing

Bring a jar of hundreds and thousands to group (or some other sweet which it is easy to get a lot of). Alternatively you can use coloured stars. Think about what would happen if every week different people found out how great it is to follow Jesus.

1. Start off with just one of the sweets on its own and the rest in a pile. The single sweet represents someone who loves Jesus.

2. Then, in week 1, this person tells one friend about how wonderful it is to know Jesus. This friend gives their life to Jesus – move over one sweet from the pile to the single sweet.

3. In week 2, these two people tell two more people (one each) about Jesus and they decide to follow Jesus – move two sweets from the pile so there should now be four sweets where there were previously two.

4. In week 3, these four people tell four more people about Jesus – move four sweets over.

5. In week 4, these eight people tell eight more people about Jesus – move eight sweets over.

Carry this on up to 10 weeks. It all starts when we tell just one of our friends about Jesus.

616. What Do You Know?

Most non-Jews who have a view about Israel will see her as a nation who is always using heavy military force against the Palestinians. Teach about Israel and God's plan for it as a nation. When Israel is next in the news the group members, by being informed of what the Bible says, will be in a position to open up conversations about God.

617. Discuss and Share

Get the group to talk about different times when they have shared Jesus with their friends. What was it like? What happened? Remember if they led their friends to Jesus to find out what happened next – how were they helped to move on with God?

618. Family Witness

Find out whose parents are Christians and whose parents are not Christians in the group.

For those with parents who are not yet Christians: Discuss how honouring their parents and praying for them will help show them that Jesus is real.

For those with parents who are Christians: Discuss how each group member can be a witness to their friends by honouring their parents.

619. I Decided to Give My Life to Jesus Because . . .

Get each person to finish off the sentence: "I decided to give my life to Jesus because …" Try to encourage them to share what brought them to the point of knowing they needed Jesus, rather than just giving a theologically correct answer. By giving a heartfelt reason, they will be in a place to share something that is real to them. Of course it also needs to be theologically correct; if there is anyone who does not clearly understand what Jesus has done for them use this as an opportunity to share it with them.

Role Play

620. My Testimony

Let the group share their testimonies with each other. How did they get saved? What has God done for them and through them? This will prepare them to be able to share with others.

621. Serve Each Other

Tell every member of the group that they have to find a way to serve somebody else in the group in the next few minutes. Afterwards explain that we can show people love by serving them at school or wherever we are.

622. My Springboard

Take any of the Ten Commandments and use them as a springboard to create opportunities to share the Gospel (do it as a role play). The role play may start by asking if the person has kept any of the Ten Commandments and move on to how God will judge them (guilty or not guilty) based on these laws. Then speak of God's grace in totally forgiving us.

623. No Talking!

Get the group to preach the Gospel to each other – but without using any words.

624. Puppet Evangelism

Bring some puppets to group and use them to talk about sharing the members' faith. Let the group then use the puppets to share with others in the group.

625. Go Against the Flow

Get the children to role play different situations they have struggled with in their school. It may be words people have said or things their friends have tried to make them do. From the role plays, encourage them to stand up and be different.

626. Use It

Model to the group how they can use a tract to spread the Gospel.

Tracts can be used to sow the first seed ("Read this and tell me what you think …");

or to work through with somebody ("Tell me what you think of this …");

or to follow up on a conversation ("After all we've been talking about you may be interested in reading this …").

Role play in the group to show them how to use different tracts in different ways. Give them some tracts to use with their friends this week.

627. Sinner's Prayer

Let the group role play leading someone to Christ, praying the sinner's prayer with each other.

628. Basics Course

Practise using a Christian Basics course such as Get Ready or God at Work (see www.childrencan.co.uk for more details) for the children to use to evangelize or take the first discipleship steps with their friends.

629. Rehearse It

Let the group practise sharing the Good News with each other, perhaps using the first week of Get Ready or God at Work as a guide.

630. Role Play

Get the group to practise sharing the Gospel with each other. Focus on the point where it is time for them to invite their friends to make a decision to go for Jesus. You can model to them first how to do this.

631. Respond

Get the group to role play sharing the Gospel with their friends and then going on to lead them to Jesus.

Witness

632. Fishing

Bring a stick with a piece of string and a small hook tied to it, or other pretend fishing rod, and some pretend fish to the group. Get them to fish for the fish one at a time. Encourage them to go and win their friends to Jesus, one friend at a time.

633. Make A Stand for the Truth

Get the group to stand in a circle with one person in the middle. The person in the middle should try to share the Gospel, while the people round the outside shout whatever they want to. The person in the middle should try and keep sharing the Gospel until you tell them to stop. Let several people have a go at standing in the middle – explain to the group that they may feel like they are alone in speaking out, with others against them, when they are sharing the Gospel, but they should keep on sharing nonetheless.

634. Being Jonah

Get different people to pretend to be Jonah speaking to the people in Nineveh – what will they say and how will they say it? What can this teach us about telling our friends about Jesus?

635. 30 Seconds

Tell the group that they have been involved in a terrorist attack. There are only 30 seconds left before everyone around them will die. They know that they are going to heaven but in those 30 seconds they need to give others an opportunity to accept Jesus. What will they say?

636. Using the Gift of Healing

Talk about how the gift of healing can be used in evangelism. Explain how the group members can pray for someone who is sick, then model to them how they can pray for their friends, by praying for anyone who is not feeling well today. Encourage them to pray for their friends at school when they are not feeling well.

637. I Will Share Jesus

Break the group up into pairs and have them take it in turns to share their own testimony. They are practising telling their friends about Jesus. Challenge them to share their testimony with a non-Christian friend this week.

Witness

On the Streets

638. Stand Up

Talk about things that are wrong in the world. After some discussion they will hopefully come up with something specific that they all feel strongly about. Encourage them to take action by writing a letter to the relevant people – this may be a politician or a regulatory body for advertising, for example.

639. Prayer-directed Evangelism

A street-evangelism team noticed that one member of the team led every person he spoke to, to Jesus. "How do you do it?" they asked. The answer was simple: "I pray and ask God to show me who He wants me to speak to, and what He wants me to say. Then I do what He tells me to." This prayer-directed evangelism should be something we do in school.

640. Impact the Community

Impact the community. Think about how you can help different groups of people in the community (the elderly, homeless, parents, etc.). Then go and do it.

641. Questionnaire

Get the group to make up a questionnaire that they can then take to others, asking questions about their beliefs and the end of time. Take the questionnaire onto the streets, to those passing by. This could be the start of an evangelistic conversation. (Don't forget to get permission from parents/guardians first!)

642. Park Evangelism

Go out as a group to the park and share your faith with those whom you see. Don't forget to get the permission of parents/guardians!

When You Get Home

643. Text 'Em

Work out some texts that the group could send to their friends. They may be snappy one-liners to get them thinking or they may be a word from God. Send the texts today (or whenever you all next get credit on your phones …!).

644. In Your Facebook

Find out what social-networking sites or websites your group members visit. Encourage them to use these sites evangelistically, to reach out to their friends.

645. Letter to A Friend

Encourage each person to write a letter to their unsaved friends, to encourage them and to help them on their journey to meeting Christ. Then let them seal it and give it to their friends.

646. Lend A Book

Encourage the group members to lend a Christian book that has had an impact on them to a non-Christian friend, then ask the friend what they thought about it.

647. The Tough One

Ask the group who the hardest person in the school is – the one least likely to get saved. Encourage them to target this person with their prayers and their witness. Back them in prayer as they do this. After all, if God could change Saul to Paul He can change those who we consider to be a hopeless case.

Witness

648. Power Prayer

Encourage each group member to prepare their hearts to be used powerfully by God. Then during the week they should look for one person to pray a power prayer for – a prayer that only God can answer (e.g. supernatural healing). They should ask for the person's permission to pray for them, then pray and watch God answer.

649. Step Out

Encourage the group members to ask their teachers for permission to take an assembly, or a tutor time, so they can share something about their faith.

650. Gather the Christians

Encourage your group to gather together with their Christian friends in their school, to pray and to witness to the rest of the school.

651. Jesus Is the Answer

Encourage everyone to find out a prayer need from one of their friends who they want to see saved. Then as a group believe God together for that prayer to be answered.

652. Faith-filled Prayers

Get each person to choose a friend who they want to see saved that week; encourage them to pray daily for their friend's salvation as well as to look for an opportunity to share with their friend. Make sure they report back on how things went the following week.

653. What Happens Next?

Set a scenario of someone beginning to share the Gospel with their friend. Ask the group what happens next. Their answer to this question will tell you whether they are full of fear or faith. Get them to pray then set the same scenario and see if things change for the better. Keep going until they leave filled with faith that their friends will be saved.

Witness

654. Wooden Cross

Give each member of the group a wooden cross and some tracts. They can wear the cross every day of the week. When people ask them about it they can tell them a bit about Jesus and give them a tract.

655. Fruitful Checklist

Work together to create a checklist of each of the aspects of the fruit of the Spirit. Each day, the children should tick off the aspects they have shown that day to see if they have demonstrated them all.

656. Receive the Holy Spirit

Pray for your group members that they will be filled with the Holy Spirit and be made bold to share the Gospel, just as occurred at Pentecost.

657. The Challenge

Set the group a challenge – to win one friend to Jesus in the next week. Get them to ask God who it should be and what they need to do. Write down the name and follow up on it in the week and at the next group meeting.

658. Questionnaire

As a group, prepare a questionnaire that the group members can use in their schools to tell people about Jesus. Get them to talk about the kinds of questions they will actually ask. The following week you can look at the results of the questionnaire and decide on the next steps.

659. Using Words of Knowledge

Talk about how a word of knowledge can be used in evangelism. Give the group an opportunity to hear from God during the group time, so that they can get used to hearing His voice.

Witness

660. Testimony

A testimony is telling others of something
that has happened that you saw, heard or experienced.
Look for an opportunity to tell someone who does
not believe in Jesus one of the reasons why you believe
in Jesus. Tell of a change that you have experienced
because of Jesus.

661. Share It

Many of the children and young people own
MP3 players or other music devices. If they are allowed
to take it to school encourage them to take in some of
your Christian music and share it with non-Christian
friends, especially the three they are praying for. If they
are not allowed to take in music players then they can
lend the music to a friend to play at home and tell
them what they thought about it.

662. I Will Share Jesus

Send the children on a secret mission in their
home. Encourage them to invite non-Christians home for
some fun. They may choose to watch a video, or simply
play with toys. During this time they should look for
opportunities to share their belief in Jesus. Don't forget
to let them report back the following week on how their
mission went.

Witness

Special Events

663. Home Cinema

Give each member of the group an evangelistic film to show to their friends. They can follow this simple, three-step plan:

1. Invite their friends.
2. Press 'Play' on the DVD player.
3. Watch their friends get saved.

Suitable films include *The Jesus Quest* (Agape Ministries, Ltd): great for children, telling the story of Jesus from a child's perspective, with a clear altar call at the end; *The Climb* (Worldwide Pictures): suitable for teenagers – covers real-life issues, with great symbolism of Jesus' sacrifice in the Gospel. Includes a scene where it is all brought together as one of the key characters is led to Christ.

664. Party

Work together to plan a party to reach out to the group's friends. Give each member a different task. Pray and invite friends!

665. Target It

Talk together as a group and prayerfully decide on a target of how many people you want to see saved this month. Work together to make a target thermometer that you can fill in as the group members (and you) lead people to Jesus.

666. Plan It

Work together to plan an evangelistic event as a group. This may build towards a special church event, or it may be an event just for the group.

667. Evangelistic Food

Get the group to talk about different foods which can be used to share the Gospel, then bring the food the next week to share together (remembering to check for allergies). Encourage the children to use the food in school in the same way. E.g. Heart-shaped sweets may talk of God's love.

668. Every Person

Get the group to think of creative ways in which they could share something of Jesus with *every* person in their school. Encourage them to step out and do these things. For example they might choose to give each person a card about Jesus or, with permission from teachers, they could put up posters in the school.

669. Mass Evangelism

Challenge the group to share the Gospel with the whole school at the same time. Discuss creative ways they can do this and start to work on these plans together.

670. Park Event

Run an event in the park at a time that is best for the group members to invite their friends to. Plan it in group time together so that each person takes responsibility for bringing along a friend.

671. Make A Movie

Get the group to make a short film, using a portable video camera, to invite their friends to group. This project will take several weeks or even months to pull together but will be worth it in the end when the group feel like they have achieved something they can show to their friends. Remember to get permission from parents and guardians if the children are to feature in the film.

672. Come Follow Me

Work together as a group to create a special drama that the children can then invite their friends to see.

673. Track the Invitations

Ask the young people how many of their friends they have invited to the next church event. Track this on a chart in the build-up to the event and get the group to share the responses from their friends each week. As they do this, set goals and pray together to believe God for a harvest.

Witness

Seasonal

674. Gearing up for School

Talk together and brainstorm ideas for evangelism as your group prepares to start a new school year – the first week back at school is the best week to begin.

675. Invitation

Encourage each member of the group to invite at least one person to a Christmas event (they may not all come, but the challenge is to invite them).

676. Christmas Party

This is the season for parties. As a group, invite friends to a Christmas party and share the Gospel as part of the programme.

677. Christmas Cards

Get the group to make evangelistic Christmas cards (or to take ordinary Christmas cards and make them evangelistic by the words they write in them).

678. Christmas Time

Talk about how we can use Christmas as a time for reaching out to our friends with the Gospel. Role play some possible scenarios.

679. Halloween Special

Talk about how we can use Halloween
as a time for reaching out to our friends with the Gospel
(not pushing them away).

680. Easter is Coming

With Easter just around the corner build
up to an Easter event being held in the church or in your group.

681. The Christmas Story

Make a booklet together to share the story of Jesus and the
purpose of His birth.

682. Carol Singing

Go carol singing as a group. Take Gospel tracts
with you, so that you can share the Gospel as
you sing together. Ensure that parents and
guardians give permission for this and that you
have the necessary ratio of adults to children.

683. The True Meaning of Christmas

Make Christingles that the group can take to school and share with their friends or in class
to demonstrate the true meaning of Christmas.

A Christingle is an orange into which are placed four fruits or sweets held in place with
cocktail sticks. It is used to illustrate God's love for the world. 'Christingle' means 'Christ Light'
– the orange represents the world; the sticks represent the four seasons; the fruit (or
sweets) represent the fruits of creation (and possibly the fruits of the Spirit). A red ribbon
around the orange signifies Jesus' death and God's all-encompassing love. Resurrection hope
and Christ as the Light of the World are symbolised by the candle in the centre.

Art and Craft

684. Map of Salvation

Draw out a map of all the people who you are in contact with and whether, as far as you know, they are saved or not. Over this term aim to see these people move along the map to salvation. The older the group the more complex you can make the map. For example you can include areas on the map such as 'Never spoken with about God', 'Speak to them regularly', 'Praying for them daily', 'Not yet praying for them regularly', and so on.

685. You Are Special

Make cards for friends that explain how much Jesus loves them. In the card, include the words 'Jesus loves YOU' and stick in a piece of tinfoil so that the person receiving the card will be able to see their own reflection when they open it.

686. Message from God

Make little cards with messages from God inside each one. Each message should be a piece of Scripture; the group can pray over what Scripture to write, and who to give each card to.

687. Special-event Focus

Get the group to make invitations and encourage them to commit to inviting their friends to the next church event suitable for their age group.

688. Opportunity Knocks

Explain how God gives us opportunities daily for sharing the Gospel in all kinds of different ways. Encourage the children to pray at the start of each day: "God, show me the opportunities you give me to share your Gospel and give me the courage to take them." Write this prayer on cards and let the children decorate them to use as a daily prayer.

689. Salvation Diary

Create a group salvation diary in which
you can record each person who the group leads to the Lord.
As you record each one let the group celebrate together
how God is using them. Keep praying for each person whom
they have led to the Lord.

690. Committed

Get the group to make commitment
cards for their friends, leaving the names blank to be filled
in later as their friends are saved. They can then pray for
their friends to be saved.

691. Evangelistic Tract

Write a tract together as a group. Decorate it
with pictures from wrapping paper.

692. The Wordless Book

Get the group to make a wordless book. Challenge them to share it with
their friends in the week. This book consists of five pages, each page
with just one colour on it. The colours tell a story as follows:

- Black – All people have sinned. Sin came into the world.

- Red – Jesus died on the cross, His blood was shed for everybody.

- White – Jesus takes away all of our sin and makes us clean again.

- Green – We then have a new life with God and we need to keep on
  growing with God.

- Gold – One day we will go to heaven, where the streets are paved
  with gold, to be with Jesus.

693. Cave Painting

Get the group to make a cave
painting, all in pictures, of the history of the world.

694. Prayer Cards

Design and develop prayer cards together to
help the group pray every day for their
evangelism of three.

Witness

695. Salesman's Pitch

If you had a product to sell that was good how would you do it? For example, how would you sell Nike trainers? Think about how you can package the Good News of Jesus making a way for us to get to God. Get the group to act on these ideas over the course of the following weeks.

696. Slogans

Let each group member make a badge to wear. The badge should encourage evangelistic discussions. For example:

- Want to know the meaning of life?
- The world's in a mess but I'm okay.
- Don't know where to turn? Ask me for directions.
- Ask me why I'm happy.
- God is good.
- I met someone great on Sunday.

Encourage the group to wear the badge every day of the week and see what conversations are started.

697. Story Time

Get the group to write the Gospel as a story, illustrate it and make a storybook that they can then give out to their friends.

698. Express It

As a group create a series of facial expressions that tell the whole Gospel story, in order. They may be happy, when Adam and Eve are created; sad, at the fall; angry, with God's judgement, and so on.

699. Show It, Don't Hide It

Get the group to make a badge with a Christian sign on it and the words "Ask me why I'm wearing this". Encourage them to wear the badge around their school and be willing to answer people who ask them the question.

Witness

700. Write It

Get the group to write a letter
to a friend who does not know Jesus, telling them
why they should get to know God. When they get
home they should give the letter to that friend.

701. Make It And Take It

Get the children to make a Jonah storybook so that they can
tell their friends the story of Jonah. Get them to practise using
it on each other as a way of sharing what God is like. Older
children should also be able to compare Jesus' death to Jonah
in the whale and so share the whole Gospel.

702. Share the Cross

Most children, preteens and teens, like to
draw. Encourage them to use their drawing skills to tell
others about Jesus. For example, every time they are with
their friends they can start to draw lots of crosses on
paper (not on school property or on public buildings!). If
people ask why they are doing it the children will have an
opportunity to share why the cross is so important to
them and what their friends need to do to accept Jesus.

703. See the Cross

Make crosses of different colours and
get the children to pin a different one to their shirt each
day. When people ask them what the cross is about, they
can then tell their friends what Jesus has done for them.

Witness